FREEDOM, EQUALITY, COMMUNITY

Freedom, Equality, Community

The Political Philosophy of Six Influential Canadians

JAMES BICKERTON, STEPHEN BROOKS,
ALAIN-G. GAGNON

McGill-Queen's University Press
Montreal & Kingston · London · Ithaca

ISBN-13: 978-0-7735-2975-5 ISBN-10: 0-7735-2975-6 (cloth)
ISBN-13: 978-0-7735-3034-8 ISBN-10: 0-7735-3034-7 (paper)

Legal deposit first quarter 2006
Bibliothèque nationale du Québec

Printed in Canada on acid-free paper that is 100% ancient forest free (100% post-consumer recycled), processed chlorine free.

This book has been published with the help of grants from St Francis Xavier University, the Université du Québec à Montréal, and the University of Windsor.

McGill-Queen's University Press acknowledges the support of the Canada Council for the Arts for our publishing program. We also acknowledge the financial support of the Government of Canada through the Book Publishing Industry Development Program (BPIDP) for our publishing activities.

Library and Archives Canadian Cataloguing in Publication

Bickerton, James
Freedom, equality, community: the political philosophy of six influential Canadians/James Bickerton, Stephen Brooks, Alain-G. Gagnon.

Includes bibliographical references and index.
ISBN-13: 978-0-7735-2975-5 ISBN-10: 0-7735-2975-6 (bnd)
ISBN-13: 978-0-7735-3034-8 ISBN-10: 0-7735-3034-7 (pbk)

1. Political science – Canada – Philosophy. 2. Canada – Politics and government – 20th century. I. Brooks, Stephen, 1956– II. Gagnon, Alain-G. (Alain-Gustave), 1954– III. Title.
JC253.B52 2006 320'.01 C2005-905814-5

Typeset in Sabon 10.5/13
by Infoscan Collette, Quebec City

Contents

Preface

It may be due to a Canadian sense of modesty, or perhaps to centuries spent as a colonial outpost of great empires, but Canadians have not been inclined to look upon themselves as important players on the world intellectual stage. They appear to themselves to be off to the side, given a line now and then, but generally destined to be supporting cast to the great centres of Western thought. Indeed, for most of Canada's history it has been normal for Canadians and *Canadiens* to go abroad, especially to England, France, and the United States, to study under the world's acknowledged experts in history, economics, literature, the sciences, and other domains of learning. In addition to being an importer of capital to build its railways, finance its factories, and develop its natural resources, Canada has been an importer of ideas.

There is nothing wrong, least of all in the world of ideas, with learning from others and importing the best of what is on offer. In this sense Canadians were enthusiastic globalists long before globalization entered the lexicon. But long years of turning their eyes outward may have caused Canadians to neglect what was growing in their own backyard and to assume that made-in-Canada, at least in the realm of ideas, signified something parochial, probably derivative, and almost certainly second-rate.

Whatever else one might say of it, Canadian political thought is none of these things. At the same time it is only fitting, and certainly very Canadian, to acknowledge the truth: the rest of the world knows little of the intellectual traditions that have evolved in Canada and Quebec and, not surprisingly therefore, the impact of Canadian thinkers and their ideas beyond their country's borders has been marginal, at best. There were no Jeffersons, Madisons, and Paines in Canada's early history. The twentieth century produced far more in Canada in the way of searching political reflection. But it may be that the comparative placidness of the Canadian scene and the gradualism of the country's evolution from colony to independent state, combined with the fact that Canada no sooner moved out from under the shadow of one fading world power, Great Britain, than it came under the shadow of an ascendant one, the United States, caused the world to pay scant attention to the political thought of Canadians and Québécois. Until the relatively recent emergence of an interest in Canadian studies and Quebec studies in the United States, Great Britain, and France, interest in and knowledge of the Canadian intellectual scene were extremely limited.

Canadians, as would be expected, awoke to the significance of their own stories and intellectual traditions before the rest of the world took any notice. The past two generations of Canadians have been educated in a university system where courses and programs of study on the history, literature, politics, culture, and political thought of French and English Canada are plentiful. They have been taught that Canadians and Québécois, like other peoples, have grappled in their own ways, and in the special circumstances of their distinctive histories, with the great questions that arise from the human condition. But they remain, with relatively few exceptions, unaware of the identities and ideas of those individuals who have contributed most to the shaping of contemporary political thought in their country.

This book is written for anyone who wishes to know more about those whose ideas have helped fashion the modern landscape of Canadian and Québécois political thought. In some cases their influence has been chiefly indirect, through writings and teaching that shaped the thinking of political decision-makers and opinion-leaders. In others, particularly in the case of Pierre Trudeau and André Laurendeau, their influence was more direct and their style more *engagé*. The six thinkers discussed in this book certainly are not the only figures to leave their mark on the political thought of French and English Canada in recent decades, but their importance is undeniable.

Acknowledgments

It is our pleasure to thank the many people who supported us in the writing and publication of this book.

Huron University College provided Stephen Brooks with an ideal atmosphere to work on portions of this book while he was a visiting research scholar. The opportunity to present some of this material to colleagues there was very much appreciated. Jim Bickerton would like to extend a note of thanks to the Department of Political Science at St Francis Xavier University for its collegial and supportive atmosphere, and to departmental secretary Marcy Baker for her cheerful and patient efficiency. Alain-G. Gagnon wishes to thank his graduate students at McGill and later at UQAM for several exchanges on the general theme of the book over the years, but especially Fred Appel, Raffaele Iacovino, Dimitrios Karmis, and Luc Turgeon.

Our universities provided welcome financial and word processing support for this project. We would like to express our special thanks to Cecil Houston, dean of Arts and Social Science at the University of Windsor, Mary McGillivray, academic vice-president at St Francis Xavier University, and Diane Demers, vice-dean, Faculty of Political Science and Law, Université du Québec à Montréal.

The people at McGill-Queen's University Press were a pleasure to work with. Roger Martin, acquisitions editor at McGill-Queen's, was unflagging in his support and a constant source of good humour during the review process. Joan McGilvray, coordinating editor, guided this book through the production process with her usual deft touch. Kate Merriman's sharp copy editing eye and judgment saved us from many infelicitous turns of phrase and obscure meanings. Luc Turgeon provided a fine index. Last, but never least, McGill-Queen's Executive Director Philip Cercone's support for this book is acknowledged with gratitude.

As always, spouses and children deserve the authors' collective acknowledgment for their sustaining love, understanding, and forbearance; Theresa MacNeil and Neil, Ben, and Luke Bickerton, Louiselle Lévesque and Vincent Gagnon, and Christine, Paul, Tom, and Marianne Brooks.

FREEDOM, EQUALITY, COMMUNITY

CHAPTER ONE

Ideas, Intellectuals, and Canadian Political Life

Ideas have often seemed elusive in Canadian politics. A century ago, the French social scientist, André Siegfried, commented on what he believed to be the almost complete absence of grand ideas and ideological conflict from Canadian politics. Instead of offering voters competing sets of ideas and waging battle over matters of principle, Siegfried said, "Canada's parties and politicians engaged in a sort of bidding war for the votes of citizens. The promise of a road, a post office, or a contract substituted for serious discussion of larger issues concerning the ends of governance." "Whoever may be the winner," Siegfried observed, "everyone knows that the country will be administered in the same way ... the only difference will be in the personnel of government" (Siegfried [1906] 1966, 113).

Siegfried has not been alone in arguing that ideas have had a hard time rising to the surface of Canadian political life, remaining submerged under heavy layers of patronage, brokerage-style party politics, and political leadership that sought to dull their edge rather than allow them to cut clean divisions through the body politic. Echoing the judgment of many of his mid-twentieth century contemporaries, the historian Frank Underhill once remarked that "Canadian history is dull as ditchwater and our politics is full of it" (Underhill 1960, 43). Commenting on the leadership style of

Canada's longest-serving prime minister, William Lyon Mackenzie King, the constitutionalist and poet F.R. Scott wrote:

> He blunted us.
>
> We had no shape
> Because he never took sides,
> And no sides
> Because he never allowed them to take shape.
>
> He seemed to be in the centre
> Because we had no centre,
> No vision
> To pierce the smoke-screen of his politics.
> (Scott and Smith 1957, 27–8)

For all that Siegfried found the apparent absence of ideas from Canadian politics to be disconcerting, he offered a charitable and functionalist explanation for what he saw as the uninspiring and even low tone of Canadian political life. Important divisions and great issues were latent in Canadian politics, he believed, but the mobilization of citizens and interests around these divisions – particularly religious and linguistic conflict – would threaten the political system to its foundations, unleashing passions and resentments that the young country might not be able to withstand. The domination of Canadian politics by two parties, Liberal and Conservative, whose principles were very similar and behaviour in office nearly identical, and the systematic refusal of Canada's leading politicians to engage one another on the battlefield of ideas, represented the price that had to be paid in order to maintain the survival of a country where great passions and ideological division lay seething below the generally dull surface of Canadian political life.

A less charitable but equally functionalist interpretation of the relative absence of grand ideas from Canadian politics was furnished by the Canadian left from about the 1950s and 1960s, in response to the failure of Canada's party system to develop along the class-based lines predicted by many social scientists. When the expected development did not occur, many on the left argued that the dominant parties, the Liberal and Progressive Conservative parties, deliberately avoided issues involving class conflict, preferring to frame Canadian politics in the familiar terms of regional and linguistic interests. In so doing these dominant parties and their leaders impeded what those on the left considered to be the normal evolution of politics in a modern society, what they called a "creative politics" that would be based on the opposing interests of workers and the owners of capital, the weak versus the privileged, and that would necessarily require that politics address such ideologically charged matters as the role of the state versus that of markets, the appropriate division of wealth in society, and the meaning of justice and equality. Creative politics would give rise to a party system polarized on class lines, providing citizens with real choices between competing sets of ideas and policies, in the process flushing what Underhill called the "ditchwater" from Canadian political life.

In their book *Crisis, Challenge and Change: Party and Class Revisited*, Janine Brodie and Jane Jenson updated the idea that ideological division has been suppressed in Canada by established parties who see in class-based politics a threat to their dominance (1988). They argued that Canada's major parties had provided citizens with a non-class definition of political life that stunted the emergence of class consciousness. Instead, voters were offered a definition of politics that purported to be pragmatic and a reflection of the mainstream values of Canadian society. The brokerage-politics style of the Liberal and Progressive Conservative parties has been, they argue, inimical to a politics of ideas (unless one considers a choice between a jobs project in New Brunswick and a government contract for a company in Mississauga to fall within the realm of ideas).

If Canada's historically dominant parties have preferred to fight it out within familiar and narrow confines, avoiding wherever possible the sorts of questions and issues those on the left believe are the real stuff of political life, this does not mean that ideas could not have entered Canadian political life through some other door. The media, academe, unions, social movements, and minor parties may identify and frame issues in alternative ways, broadening the discourse of politics beyond the preferred parameters of the dominant parties and their leaders and injecting ideas into political life. There is no doubt that this has happened in Canada. Moreover, the Canadian left's argument that the only idea-based conflict deserving of the name is that which is based on class is flawed. The classic faultlines of Canadian politics – French v. English, Canada v. the

United States, and central Canada v. the eastern and western regions of the country – are associated with ideas about the country, the nature of Canadian society, the proper interpretation of its history, and normative judgments on that history. None of this can be reduced to a mere by-product of class conflict.

It would be strange, indeed, for a society to give rise to great ideas concerning issues that are not essential to its history. The work of great thinkers arises from the ferment of the conditions that characterize their society. One would expect intellectuals, senior politicians, and opinion-leaders to turn their attention to the defining faultlines of Canadian history and the Canadian condition, and to interpret more universal questions involving freedom, equality, justice, and human dignity in terms of this history and these conditions.

The preoccupations of Canada's leading intellectuals are, indeed, what one would expect from the history of the country. It is probably fair to say that Canadians and Québécois have talked and written about ethnolinguistic division and the proper understanding of the history of relations between Frenchand English Canada as much as the intellectuals of any other linguistically divided society. Canada's relationship to the United States is so intimately woven into the Canadian consciousness and has inspired such an enormous outpouring of analysis and polemic that no telling of the Canadian story can avoid reflecting on the meaning and consequences of this relationship. Indeed, the ways in which English Canadian intellectuals have thought and talked about freedom, equality, and community – the thematic pillars of this book – have been powerfully influenced by perceptions of Canada's southern neighbour. The nature of the relationship between what has often been called the industrial heartland of Canada, stretching from Windsor to Montreal, and the less populous regions to the east and west of this corridor, has been ignored by some of Canada's leading political thinkers whose attention has been fixed on questions arising from French-English and Can-Am relations. Nevertheless, some of the best history writing, such as that of Harold Innis and Donald Creighton, has understood the importance of the regional question for an understanding of the Canadian condition.

BYSTANDERS TO HISTORY?

Contrary to what Siegfried and many others have suggested, Canadian political life has not been bereft of grand ideas. Even Mackenzie

King, who did as much as any single person to keep ideas and ideological conflict out of Canadian political life, made his small contribution to the stockpile of Canadian political thought through the corporatist vision elaborated so ponderously in his book *Industry and Humanity* (1918). In a country whose history has been marked by deep and often passionate divisions – between Catholics and Protestants in the early history of Canada, and between French and English Canada for all of the country's history – where regional resentments have long simmered and frequently boiled over to produce parties of protest, and where the country's relationship to the United States has been a source of controversy and angst for over two centuries, ideas could not be excluded from political life.

Siegfried may have overstated the case, although in his defence it must be said that Canadian public life during the first several decades after Confederation was not notable for the presence of high principles or inspiring political leaders. Railroads, tariffs, and squabbles between the centralizing designs of the Conservative Party, led by John A. Macdonald, and the forces defending provincial rights in the fledgling country were the dominant public issues of the times. Canada's relationship to Great Britain occasionally provided the impetus for broader reflection on the nature of the country and its future, as occurred during the Boer War and again during World War I, and the Great Depression of the 1930s spawned a wave of critical rethinking about capitalism and the appropriate role of government through the Cooperative Commonwealth Federation – predecessor to the New Democratic Party – the League for Social Reconstruction, intellectual organs like the *Canadian Forum*, and even among many establishment politicians and leading bureaucrats[1]. But the broad centre of Canadian politics, represented by the Liberal and Conservative parties, continued along in the brokerage-politics mode of avoiding direct engagement with ideas and principles in preference for interests and patronage. Grand reflection on policy and the role of government tended to be managed through that most Canadian of devices, the royal commission, and its near cousin, the policy white paper. These bureaucratized and state-controlled methods for critically examining some aspect of Canadian society, economics, or public policy provided what, from the standpoint of state elites, has surely seemed a politically safe channel for consideration of new ideas in public life. To some degree they have performed a function that might otherwise have been expected to be filled by the party system and elections.[2]

It is usual to attribute the low profile that ideas have had in Canadian public life to such factors as the party system; the impact of federalism, which has transformed issues that might have been framed in terms of grand ideas and principles into questions of jurisdiction; and the political culture, which is less polarized on class lines than in many other western democracies. But to some degree the explanation may lie in the fact that Canada has always been, nationalist pretences aside, a bystander to world history. The Americans, the French, and the British, to name a few, all shaped the course of world history in their various ways. Their domestic struggles and their international involvements gave rise to critical reflection on their principles of government. Senior politicians and leading thinkers were aware that their nation was a force in shaping history and, therefore, that the consequences of their ideas and actions would not be light and transient.

Canada, by contrast, developed on the margins of history's march, seen by the rest of the world as that place north of the United States. Without meaning to diminish the importance for those involved of the domestic struggles and accomplishments that have marked Canadian history, these struggles and accomplishments have not been of an order that captured the outside world's attention. It should come as little surprise, therefore, that Canadians' reflections on their politics and society, and on the human condition as viewed through a Canadian lens, have had little impact beyond this country's borders. On the contrary, Canadians historically have been enthusiastic importers of ideas fashioned elsewhere, adapting them to Canadian circumstances, but exporting little intellectual capital in return. (It must be said, however, that Canada has long been an exporter of intellectuals and creative people generally, although this is not the same thing as exporting distinctively Canadian ideas.)

Some would argue that this is no longer the case and that, in recent decades, Canada has moved from the margins of history toward its centre, showing other countries how a multi-cultural society based on principles of tolerance, equality, and respect for group rights can be made to work. Intimations of this were already to be found two generations ago in the writings of Pierre Elliott Trudeau. He argued that Canada, if it could find ways of respecting and protecting the rights of its two main ethnolinguistic communities, could provide a working example to the world of a non-ethnic form of nationhood. Since Trudeau's time, it has become common among the country's English-speaking intellectuals to argue that the evolution of group rights since the Charter of Rights and Freedoms became law in 1982 and recognition of forms of Aboriginal self-government demonstrate that Canada is fashioning a society built on pillars of tolerance and equality, showing the way for other nations. The work of such Canadians as Michael Ignatieff, Charles Taylor, and Will Kymlicka is known throughout the English-speaking world, demonstrating that Canada has emerged from its long adolescence in the world of ideas.

Whether Canada is no longer a bystander to world history is not a question that we can answer here. It is certain that the intellectuals and opinion-leaders of all societies exaggerate the importance and even awareness in the rest of the world of those issues and accomplishments that they know so intimately. If Canadians are guilty of this fault, then they are not alone. But it also seems likely that, more than in the past, the Canadian case warrants the world's attention. As global migration changes the demographic and cultural faces of societies and the forces of globalization challenge and render antiquated traditional notions of sovereignty and nationhood, the struggles that are ongoing in Canada may indeed have relevance far beyond this country's borders.

English Canadian politicians and nationalist intellectuals frequently boast that Canada is pioneering a sort of post-modern, post-nationalist form of pluralistic society where, in Charles Taylor's words, different communities can belong to Canada in different ways. Whether this is truly the future, for Canada or any other country, is far from obvious. But as Canadians attempt to cope with the complicated dynamics of their own condition, including tighter economic integration into the North American market, profound demographic changes over the last several decades as a result of a shift to non-European sources of immigration, the challenge of Aboriginal demands for greater autonomy and even sovereignty, and the continuing uncertainty of Quebec's relationship to the rest of Canada, their efforts to think through the questions raised by these forces surely resonate beyond their borders.

FREEDOM, EQUALITY, AND COMMUNITY VIEWED THROUGH THE CANADIAN PRISM

This book is an exploration of the modern political traditions of French and English Canada, viewed through the prism of some of their leading intellectuals. We have selected figures from each linguistic community whose influence on their fellow intellectuals' thinking about politics has been profound. From English Canada we have chosen Harold Innis, an economic historian, and George Grant, a philosopher whose writings on Canada have been widely read by social scientists. From French Canada we have chosen Marcel Rioux, a sociologist, and André Laurendeau, a journalist and leading nationalist intellectual of his generation. We also include Pierre Elliott Trudeau, a former prime minister and leading Quebec federalist of his generation, and Charles Taylor, a philosopher, both of whom we consider to span the French-English divide. The freedom/equality/community framework used throughout this book is intended to assist readers in making sense of each thinker in terms of concepts that are both familiar and central to democratic theory. Applying a common framework is also intended to enable readers to better discern the similarities and contrasts in the work of these leading Canadian political thinkers.

In choosing several thinkers for inclusion in this book we have been guided by a simple rule. We have selected those whose ideas, in our judgment, have most powerfully influenced the political thinking of Canadians and Québécois over the last two generations and, moreover, whose writings help us understand how Canadians have thought about some of the core values of democratic politics and their meaning in Canada. All of the thinkers included in this book – some more than others – have written extensively about the Canadian condition. Through the prism of their work we hope to arrive at an understanding of how each has conceived of the grand architecture of democratic political life – freedom, equality, and community – in the Canadian or Québécois space.

Four of the six thinkers whose work and influence are examined in this book are from Quebec. All four spent most of their adult lives in Montreal. We are aware that this may seem oddly skewed and not representative of the range of perspectives that have contributed to Canadian intellectual life. The fact that so many preeminent Canadian intellectuals and artists, individuals whose work has interpreted the Canadian experience and explored the Canadian imagination, are from Montreal can hardly be dismissed as accidental. Charles Taylor has said that Montreal, historically Canada's most bilingual city, has been a sort of estuary where the waters of French- and English-speaking Canada, and their different cultural traditions and histories, have met and mixed. It is not surprising that this meeting place of Canada's two linguistic solitudes has produced many of the country's most prominent political thinkers.

This presumes, some will object, the centrality of French-English relations to the Canadian political experience and the comparative marginality of regional perspectives from outside of central Canada and of what might be called "new Canada" perspectives that start from the fact that the Canada of today is far more ethnically pluralistic than it was a generation ago. Of the six thinkers whose ideas we examine, only Innis addresses in a major way questions of regionalism and centre-periphery relations. Of the six only Taylor weaves multiculturalism into the central pattern of his thought.

If the preoccupation and interpretation of these six thinkers appear to be predominantly central Canadian, this simply reflects the reality of Ontario and Quebec's domination of the national political stage. Had it been the case that British Columbia or Alberta or the combined Maritime provinces had a population nearly equal to that of either Ontario or Quebec, the contours of Canadian political life would have been drawn quite differently. It has, however, always been the case that central Canada had, and continues to have, the economic and political clout to thrust its concerns, interests, and visions of the country to the centre of Canada's national life. This, of course, has fuelled regional grievances and even a longstanding sense of political alienation in western Canada. It has not, however, produced much in the way of political philosophy beyond a negative philosophy of grievance expressed by someone like George Woodcock, writing from British Columbia. One searches in vain for a thinker of the stature of Laurendeau, Taylor, or Grant emerging from the experience of western or Atlantic Canada and expressing a vision of politics and of Canada that has resonated through this country's intellectual life to the same degree as the six intellectuals we have selected.

They are, of course, all white males of either Anglo-Saxon or French origin – or a mixture of the two. Thirty years from now, when someone writes this sort of book about thinkers whose ideas have helped shape the course of Canadian politics in the twenty-first century, the selection of thinkers will very likely be more inclusive. But in terms of thinkers whose work has influenced recent generations of Canadian opinion-leaders and policy-makers, we believe that most observers of the Canadian political scene would agree with our choices. Together their work reflects the key intellectual debates over Canada's most enduring and vital internal political struggle – the national unity issue – as well as its most pressing external concern – the country's relationship with the United States.

Our exploration of the ideas and influence of several prominent intellectuals from Canada's two chief language communities is not intended to be biography. Nonetheless, the experiences and individuals that shaped the thought, philosophy and careers of these leading political thinkers cannot be ignored. Ideas and the intellectual traditions they express have sources, and these sources need to be identified and explained. Consequently, some biography is necessary. But unlike such a marvellous study as Carl Berger's *The Writing of Canadian History* (1976), our principal aim is not to understand the sources of an intellectual tradition but to explain the impact of a tradition – or two traditions in this case – on politics and society.

In saying that Canada has been characterized by two intellectual traditions, one Quebecois and the other Canadian, we do not mean to suggest that this country's intellectual life has been marked by two solitudes. It is inescapably the case, however, that political thinking in French-speaking Quebec and in the rest of Canada has drawn on significantly different sources and focused attention on rather different questions and problems. Who would deny the absolute centrality of the national question in the political tradition of French-speaking Quebec? English Canada has always had its own national question which is, obviously, quite different from that of Quebec. The two traditions are, of course, linked by the fact that relations between the French- and English-speaking communities and the status of Quebec have been central concerns of both, and each tradition has evolved in response to its perception of the other. Moreover, there are important cross-over figures like Taylor and Trudeau, and to a lesser degree Laurendeau, who have had an important impact on both traditions. But the development of a Québécois identity, particularly since the Quiet Revolution, has reinforced the divide between these traditions.

The themes of freedom, equality, and community do not have equal weight in the works of the six thinkers discussed in the following chapters. Nor is it always possible, or for that matter desirable, to neatly separate these concerns in the writings of any one of them. These themes tend to be woven together in a complex skein of ideas in which one theme provides the dominant tone. For example, Charles Taylor's arguments about freedom and equality are filtered through what we would argue is a particular moral vision of community. The communal strand of Taylor's thinking suffuses his entire œuvre, giving his arguments on freedom and equality a distinctive colour. Pierre Trudeau, on the other hand, starts from quite different first premises. Trudeau's ideas regarding collective rights and nationalism are powerfully influenced by his liberal individualism. His well-known antipathy toward nationalism, and his ideas on linguistic equality, are shaped by an individualistic philosophy whose influence is evident throughout his writings and political career.

Trudeau aside, it is probably fair to say that the problem of individual freedom is not generally thought of as central to the œuvre of any of the other thinkers examined in this book, nor to Canadian political thought in general. This is, however, only partially true. Canadians have tended to conceive of freedom as a social product, a condition that is possible only in a certain kind of society with certain kinds of institutions. The book title *Freedom Wears a Crown* captures well the older Canadian notion that real freedom can only be experienced within a social order that respects stability and the rule of law. Today, Canadians continue to be deeply skeptical of American conceptions of freedom as the absence of constraint and as a sort of pre-political state that, per Locke, provides the raison d'être for government and a moral social order.

It would be somewhat misleading, however, to suggest that Canadian political thinking has assigned little weight to questions of freedom, compared to issues of equality and community. This appears to be the case only when Canada is compared to the United States. But questions associated with freedom *have* been important and the ways in which equality and community have been conceived would be incomplete and incoherent without an examination of what Canadian political thinkers have said about freedom.

Each of the six thinkers discussed in the following chapters has a defining tone to his work and occupies a distinctive place in Canadian intellectual and public life. Taken together, their writings provide a sort of map of modern Canadian and Québécois intellectual waters, at least as concerns political life. Not every school, tributary, and current is covered by this map, but someone wishing to navigate the waters of Canadian democratic thought is unlikely to be put off course by the picture that emerges from their work. They truly are six thinkers whose writings have made a difference.

CHAPTER TWO

The Radical Political Economy of Harold Innis

Harold Innis was Canada's first scholar in the social sciences to secure an international reputation. An economic historian at the University of Toronto from 1920 until his untimely death in 1952, Innis, along with W.A. Mackintosh, developed the "staples thesis," an integrative and distinctively Canadian approach to the study of economic, social, and political development in frontier societies or "white settler" colonies. In his later years, Innis extended this seminal work on the role of staples (such as fish, fur, timber, wheat, and pulp and paper) in Canadian economic history into research on the history of communications and its relationship to the rise and decline of cultures and civilizations. Described as a "singular genius" (Christian 1980, viii) and "forcefully original" (Clement 1989, 7), his ideas and insights influenced a wide range of thinkers in a variety of disciplines: economics, history, geography, sociology, political science, communications, and Canadian studies. His is one of the most important contributions (even more so because of its pervasive and often subliminal influence) to twentieth century scholarly and political debates about Canadian history, economy, society, and culture.

Unlike the other thinkers profiled in this book, Harold Innis was not a philosopher or political theorist. Nor was he an "engaged intellectual" in the sense of publicly participating in politics. His legacy is contained within scholarly writings which are difficult, dense, leaden in exposition, and not readily accessible to readers, though they tend to be, in the words of historian Donald Creighton, "interrupted by brilliant generalizations" (Creighton, 20). Innis himself, "a shy man, awkward of manners, little given to light conversation" (Clark, 29), was anything but charismatic. As for his thoughts on politics, these seemed almost purely incidental; he rarely isolated political matters from the broader social, economic, and cultural context (Berger, 100; Whitaker, 820). Indeed, Whitaker uses the description "cryptic opacity" to capture the character of Innis's political thought. In other words, fully and clearly understanding Innis as a political thinker and writer poses a significant challenge to even the most sophisticated reader.

For these reasons, Innis's influence on Canadian politics was neither direct nor immediate. Indeed, there was a noticeable discontinuity between Innis and the next generation of Canadian scholars. His methodologies and insights were neither systematically followed nor rationally criticized; his work was largely ignored, and his way of seeing Canada either significantly modified or replaced. In short, because he was avoided rather than followed, his immediate intellectual inheritance was relatively meager. (Westfall, 38)

Innis simply did not inspire a group of disciples promoting an "Innisian school"; his thought was not of the "system-creating" sort (Christian 1980). This, it seems, is precisely the way Innis would have wanted it. "He distrusted theory. He felt it often led to the creation of new dogma, new rigidities, and new monopolies of knowledge" (Clark, 29; Salter, 194). Nor did Innis attempt to insert himself into the great political issues and movements of his day. He was opposed to the idea that university scholars would directly involve themselves in politics, or otherwise place themselves at the service of political and bureaucratic masters, and he was openly disdainful of intellectuals who "sold their souls" to the state or to a partisan cause[1] (Creighton, 22; Berger, 101; Salter and Dahl, 114).

All this makes Innis very difficult to classify as a thinker. Both those who knew him personally and those who have written about him since his death have described his political and ideological orientation in various, sometimes contradictory ways: he was a radical conservative, a whig liberal, a nationalist and an anti-nationalist, an anti-imperialist who extolled the merits of certain types of empire, an anti-modernist, an anti-centralist, a technological and geographic determinist, an unrelenting materialist, and "an individual in revolt against mass society" (Clement, 8). Though no one has asserted that Innis himself was a socialist, and most agree that at best his nationalism was provisional (Acland, 251), his work has been used by both socialists and nationalists to argue their respective (and sometimes overlapping) positions. Finally, at the end of the twentieth century, a new generation of communication theorists has embraced the insights embedded within his later work on communications and culture, describing them as profound and path-breaking.

Above all else, Harold Innis was an intellectual who embraced the perspective of the marginalized and the colonized, who recognized the uneven but reciprocal power relationship that existed between the centre and the margin within empires (whether political, economic, or cultural), as well as the social dislocation and contradictory effects that always attended economic and technological change.

In almost all of its facets, Innis's work was distinctively Canadian. The greater part of his academic career was devoted to developing a philosophy of economic history that was suited to Canadian needs. In creating the staples thesis to fill this void, he helped reorganize the way Canada was understood as a nation, while providing a new raison d'être for the existence of the Canadian state (Westfall, 37). He examined the origins of Canada's reliance on natural resources (or "staples"), and explained its relationship to economic dependence and to regionalism, as well as its shaping effects on Canadian political, economic, and social institutions. Innis was also highly critical of and deeply concerned about the growing sway of American commercialism over Canada in the postwar period, the cultural struggle for survival this implied for English Canada, and the disconnection it was likely to engender (or exacerbate) between English and French Canada (Acland, 250). This alarm about the cultural 'swamping' of English Canada by an aggressively expansionist American empire – and what effects this might have on the social and political stability of Canadian society – was powerfully echoed in the later work of both George Grant and Marcel Rioux.

It is these enduring Canadian themes that are present throughout Innis's work: dependence and development, imperial-colonial (or centre-margin, or metropole-hinterland) relations, nationalism and regionalism, anti-Americanism. However, in distinction from the classically nationalist position on these subjects, it was not so much Canada's quasi-colonial status within an empire that concerned Innis as it was the character of that empire and the relationship between territories, peoples, and technologies inscribed within it. For instance, for Innis it was the lack of balance within the American empire, its complete and utter present-mindedness and lack of regard for history and cultural tradition that was deeply disturbing, and made him fear for Canada's future as a dependency within that empire (Christian 1977, 28; Whitaker, 327).

Innis had other concerns as well, about individual freedom and the state of those institutions and cultural practices that he saw as essential to the quality of Canadian democracy. In particular, Innis was concerned about the university and its role within society. As Canada's pre-eminent social science scholar, and as head of the influential Department of Political Economy at the University of Toronto from 1937 until his death, Innis played a lead role in determining the direction of work in the social sciences, establishing standards of scholarly excellence, founding the *Canadian Journal of Economics and Political Science*, and defending the autonomy and freedom of individual scholars and the university community (Clark, 27; Spry, 108). It was in this specific context that historian Carl Berger referred to Innis as a "prickly nationalist." "Innis tried to make universities live up to what he regarded as their duty to expand research, create Canadian scholars, and place these scholars in Canadian institutions." In doing this, Innis virtually alone created the "Toronto school" that looms so large in the historical development of the social sciences in Canada (Westfall, 38).

Academic freedom and university autonomy mattered deeply to Innis because he regarded the university as perhaps the only institution that both allowed and encouraged intellectuals to resist the social, political, and economic influences that bias the structure of knowledge (Westfall, 44). For Innis, the university was "the crowning glory of a pluralistic, democratic society" (Berger, 110). It was virtually the only setting where some perspective on bias, and therefore a greater measure of objectivity in the open-ended search for knowledge, could be gained (Salter and Dahl, 116). While every other domain was preoccupied with the present and with immediate results, "those within the university can examine bias, longer-term perspectives, and the full dimensions of public issues" (Salter and Dahl, 123). This was why Innis looked so severely on those university scholars who allowed themselves to be co-opted by government, political parties, or social movements.

For Innis, the purpose of knowledge generated and cultivated within the university was to break the stranglehold of the present.

> There was great value in what did not immediately appear relevant in relation to the needs of the present because only by the study of the past and its broad problems could the individual attain a more independent perspective on his time and on himself. To know nothing but the present was to be a helpless victim of the debased myths of one's own immediate time. Scholarship, fragile though Innis understood it to be, was the corrective to the biases of the present, and it was through the search for truth that individual freedom was enlarged. (Berger, 110)

Especially in the modern context of overwhelming media influence, intellectuals based in free and autonomous universities were one of the few counterforces to pervasive present-mindedness, and the best hope for retaining a sense of history and the oral tradition necessary to secure the balance and moderation so essential to a durable, healthy society and a creative culture. Moreover, it was crucial that "the values of university life – respect for truth, evaluations of bias, multiple perspectives, tolerance, skepticism – should be preserved and passed on to students" (Salter and Dahl, 121). This was central to the process of educating a free-thinking, democratic citizenry. Education could never be allowed to become the simple transmission of facts; real education was a process of moral and intellectual formation that facilitated independent thought. Innis was convinced this would be lost unless the university was preserved from the corrupting influences of commercialism and the state, and he fought tenaciously and unstintingly (at times as a lone voice against what seemed to be the tide of history) for this vision.

There were a number of influences in Innis's early life and academic career that helped to shape these views on humanity, society, and its institutions. Innis was born in 1894 on a farm in southwestern Ontario, the eldest son of "hardshell Baptist" parents who were devoutly religious. While Innis did not pursue a career in the ministry as his mother had hoped, he did attend two universities with Baptist connections (McMaster and the University of Chicago). In later life, Innis would reject religion but retain its focus on ethics and cling to certain convictions and values characteristic of the Baptist denomination, especially belief in the independence, dignity, and self-sufficiency of the individual. His Baptist-nurtured suspicion of and disdain for centralized bureaucracy and institutionalized authority was deepened by his military service overseas in the First World War (Creighton, 17; Stamps, 56). Plans for a legal career after the war were set aside after a summer-school experience at the University of Chicago took him on the path of a Ph.D. in economics and an academic career. After completing his thesis on the Canadian Pacific Railway, he accepted a position in the Department of Political Economy at the University of Toronto in 1920 (Creighton, 18).

During his doctoral studies Innis was particularly influenced by the thought of Thorstein Veblen, the renowned nineteenth-century American economic theorist who had been a major figure at the University of Chicago. Innis accepted Veblen's scathing critique of the static, ahistorical approach of classical and neo-classical economics, and throughout his academic life remained opposed to the type of narrow disciplinary specialization that he believed imposed fetters upon skeptical, open-ended inquiry. He continually argued for an interdisciplinary and historical approach to social science that was both holistic and culturally-specific. In this connection, he "resisted efforts to detach economics and sociology from an historically oriented social science that embraced economic history and political theory" (Clark, 31). He wanted to cultivate an exchange relationship between the traditional disciplines, "to bring a multiplicity of resources and insights to bear on relevant problems, both intellectual and practical" (Heyer, 257).

Perhaps the main criticism of Innis's work is that it often seems to exclude the very human beings that historians take as their subject. Thus, for Berger, Innis is ultimately a geographical and technological determinist whose method and approach effectively "dehumanize" Canadian history. Impersonal, inescapable, and anonymous forces simply overwhelm and reduce to insignificance the actions and choices of individuals (Berger, 93, 94, 98). Others reject this interpretation and characterization of Innis. They agree that geography constitutes a powerful structure for Innis, but one that constantly interacts with other principal economic forces such as elites, technology, primary producers, and labour markets (Drache, xxix). Moreover, while technology might "hasten," "facilitate," or "help define" the character of an historical epoch, for Innis it was never the final determinant.

> Interplay, formation and interaction ... are terms which best describe his view of the historical process. If Innis neglects the social relations of production in his communication researches, as he certainly does, and is somewhat naïve with respect to the role of ideology, he nevertheless leaves suitable openings for their inclusion as a generation of Innis-inspired researchers are beginning to demonstrate. (Heyer, 257)

Far from being crudely deterministic, the staples thesis in Innis's hands was a marvellously sophisticated and complex instrument,

> a way of examining the relationship between various elements in the historical process, especially social structure, politics, and the economic system. It located all these elements within a dynamic imperial system characterized by a disequilibrium between metropolitan centers and their hinterlands ... Staples illuminated the ties between government, business and society, and consequently linked economics to geography, political science, and sociology. And it tied all of them to the study of Canadian history. (Westfall, 39)

FREEDOM

In his various writings, Innis mounts a powerful critique of modern society, and much of this revolves around his conception of freedom, the dangers to it, and how best to preserve it. Innis's notion of freedom is derived from an older kind of liberalism rooted in the ideas of eighteenth century British philosophers such as Hume and conservative (or Whig liberal) thinkers such as Edmund Burke. For Hume and Burke freedom can only exist where the law creates it and where it is maintained by a civil culture in which individuals are protected from the arbitrary will of others. In other words, freedom is not an abstract and inalienable right of individuals that is then restricted or impinged upon by legal and political authorities, either with (democracy) or without (autocracy) their consent. Instead, freedom is understood to be a product of specific historical and cultural conditions, the result of certain customs, conventions, and institutions that have evolved over a long period of time. The presence of human freedom in a society is a measure of that society's balance and stability, which "produce conditions in which humans can flourish" (Noble, 32–4).

It was this Whig liberal or Tory conservative British tradition that shaped Canadian political culture and clearly differentiated it from that of the United States. Innis was steeped and nurtured in this cultural and political milieu, and more overtly exposed to it in his formal education. This view of freedom was also amenable to his distrust of centralized authority and bureaucracy (in effect, of institutionalized power) and his faith in the dignity, integrity, and creativity of the individual at the margins of systems of centralized social control. It affirmed for him the key role of such institutions as parliaments and legislatures, courts and the common law, and (of course) universities. These institutions protected spheres of non-interference in which the individual is free to act and served as a counterbalance to the tendency toward centralization and monopoly. It is the continued autonomy, health, and vitality of such institutions, Innis surmised, that maintains the requisite cultural balance and political stability within society that makes individual freedom possible (Noble, 39–42).

The basis for Innis's ideas about human freedom, however, went well beyond either simple intellectual agreement with earlier Whig liberal thinkers, or the cultural conditioning that would have accompanied his immersion in Anglo-Canadian values, traditions, and institutions (although undoubtedly both were relevant). It was Innis's own materialist analysis of Canadian and world history that shaped and informed his views on freedom. His various researches were most directly concerned with empires and the monopolies of power and knowledge that they invariably promote. Innis loathed monopolies of all sorts, and extended this economic concept to the spheres of politics and culture.

> There seems to be an underlying fear that runs throughout Innis's work that there is an all too disturbing tendency of social organizations to seek to control as far as possible the life of the individuals within their ambit. Implicit in Innis's writings is a preference for what Michael Oakeshott calls a civil association, a state in which autonomous and integrated individuals live in free association with others of their kind, pursuing their chosen ends in the context of rules or laws which outline the conditions of their association. It is this tendency [of monopolies] to destroy the conditions for free association that Innis deprecates. (Christian 1977, 32)

Innis's scholarly method was to analyze the structure and workings of the economic, social, and political institutions of particular empires (whether formal or informal) in order to understand the biases embedded within them. Innis responded positively to Thorstein Veblen's concern to detect what he called "trends" and to escape their influence (Berger, 88). In Innis's work, this translated into an almost obsessive preoccupation with the negative effects of "bias" and how these could be counteracted. For Innis the main task of the social scientist was to uncover and reveal the effect of bias on social institutions (Creighton, 21).

One of the fundamental lessons of history, for Innis, was that the efficient organization of markets depended upon the secular exercise of power by elites, and that control over the technology of communication was the principal lever by which this was done. Elite control over technology, wielded through large-scale organizations (religious, military, corporate, administrative), produced "monopolies of knowledge" that gave these elites control over social space and the social order. Innis analyzed the ways elites cultivated each wave of new technology in order to enhance their authority and prestige, using specialized knowledge as both an economic weapon and as an instrument of power for empires, nations, and states. (Drache, xlvi) Innis posited a certain irony in this, however, in that the more complete the monopolistic control of elites, the more vulnerable were they and their institutions (and by extension the civilizations they represented) to eventual overthrow and destruction (Christian 1977, 34).

Past civilizations had been one of two types. "Temporalizing" civilizations relied on technologies of communication (or media) that stressed orality and a strong oral tradition; they exhibited a "time bias" which favoured cultural preservation and "enhanced social cohesion by means of powerful belief systems, reinforced by family, kinship and religious ties." "Spatializing" civilizations relied on various forms of formal written text as the main technology of communication; they had a "space bias" which enhanced the capacity for political coordination and encouraged a social structure suited to the need to control far-flung regions within an empire (Drache, xlvi). The most durable, creative, and healthy civilizations were those that were characterized by cultural balance brought on by the presence of media that exhibited counteracting biases. This created a situation where elite preoccupation with political and economic control over space (territory) was countered with a cultural obsession with time (history, ethics, values, and tradition). The resulting societal balance and moderation forestalled the growth of a self-destructive monopoly of power and knowledge (ultimately the bane of civilization and individual freedom). Under these conditions human civilization – and within it individual freedom and creativity – was able, for a time, to flourish. Always, however, the central problem for Innis was one of power (be it civil or economic): who possessed power and how did its exercise impact upon the social order, and in particular the dignity and freedom of the individual? (Christian 1980, xvi)

It is this question of power, and particularly the relationship between power and knowledge, that Whitaker argues is central to Innis's later work, which was increasingly political in its orientation. Innis did not have a sanguine view of power. "Power is poison ... a friend in power is a friend lost" (Whitaker, 824). But Innis's understanding of power went well beyond its personal manifestations and effects. His scholarly interest was in the social power gained through control over knowledge and its byproducts (such as technology). Monopolistic control over communication media had the odious effect of allowing the power elite to construct a form of ideological hegemony that suppressed freedom of thought and inquiry.

> He [...] believed that the fundamental form of social power is the power to define what reality is. Monopolies of knowledge in the cultural sense refer to the efforts of groups to determine the entire world view of a people: to produce, in other words, an official view of reality which can constrain and control human action. (Carey on Innis, as quoted in Whitaker, 825)

In the modern context, the progressive mechanization and monopolization of knowledge embeds within communication media a growing bias in the direction of control over space, while simultaneously undermining those media of communication (particularly the oral tradition) that have a time bias concerned with, and capable of maintaining and transmitting, the cultural heritage of past generations. This monopolization of knowledge through space-biased media of communication implies great class inequality of political and economic power, but Innis locates the material basis for this systematic bias in thought "at a deeper level than class alone, although that is involved ... it colours all thought communicated through the same media, whatever its source" (Whitaker, 826).

The increasing pace of technological progress associated with modernity, which for many heralded the inevitable triumph of human rationality, instead caused Innis to foresee violent disturbance and ultimate civilizational collapse, brought on by a radical imbalance and instability at the centre of Western civilization. This imbalance (whereby space-biased media completely dominates time-biased media) produces both an accelerated rate of change and an exaggerated "present-mindedness" in Western culture that literally destroys time (in the sense of an appreciation of time) and along with it the intellectual capacity to bring perspective to bear on the 'here and now.' For Innis this process was catastrophic, because the ongoing mechanization of knowledge (a product of the dominance of space-biased technologies such as mass media) entailed the loss of the oral tradition (and the dialogue that is central to it) that is a core element of time-biased media. The oral tradition, Innis argued, acted as an antidote to the technological effects of modernity. It had the salutary effect of enhancing the individual's sense of continuity and community by nurturing cultural memory; it promoted empathy and thus a reverence for values and ethics; and it encouraged tolerance for ambiguity in meaning. Its loss would "lock the culture into an eternal present" (Stamps, 62–3). This would fully unleash individualism as a dynamic of change, but also leave individuals culturally and intellectually deprived and open to manipulation by controlling elites (Salter, 198).

It was only the continued possibility, however slight, that countermeasures might yet be set in motion that would restore balance in Western civilization that left "some glimmers of light amid the gathering gloom" for Innis. This hope prevented him from going beyond his stance of "radical conservatism" to a position of total pessimism and despair (Whitaker, 826). The source of this hope lay in Innis's "faith in the human spirit and in the creative and liberating power of human intelligence" (Christian, 42). It also sprang from his historical dialecticism, his belief that opposing tendencies are at work in history (Salter, 194). Thus, monopolies of knowledge are opposed by antagonistic elements working against them. This can create cracks in the façade of monopoly power that allow the "human spirit" to break through, usually on the intellectual and territorial margins of empire, "at new levels of society and on the outer fringes" (Innis as quoted in Whitaker, 826).

Innis's view of the radical potential of the margin did not accord with the well-established views of previous social and economic thinkers who argued that social change originated at the centre and emanated from there to outlying regions.

> The contrary, Innis argued, is true; it is those areas that have escaped the restrictive influences at the centre [which can be understood in both spatial and intellectual terms] that retain the possibility of development. Technology has its greatest impact in frontier areas which are more open to social change, and then works in to the centre in an attack on the more conservative elements ... Whether empires [political, commercial, military, religious] were overthrown from within or without, the agents of change would most likely be elements that had been marginal to the empire" (Christian 1980, xiii). New technologies, in other words, have often been the equivalent of double-edged swords, making possible the extension of control from the centre, while at the same time providing those on the periphery with a potential weapon of resistance (Salter, 196).

Innis's thinking about freedom, then, had a dual origin and dimension. It had older, traditional roots in a nineteenth-century Anglo-Canadian culture that was 'Whig liberal' or Tory in its values. However, it also arose from a radically new political-economy critique of technologies of communication and their relationship to monopolies of knowledge and power. The latter posed a threat to civilization and individual freedom if not in some way checked or counterbalanced. Though pessimistic about the direction of things in the postwar period, Innis still signaled some hope that the gathering momentum of an elite-dominated system of social control would not become complete, averted in the end by the resilience and resistance of individuals and communities on the margins of empire whose creative adoption and use of new technologies ultimately would forestall (if not directly undermine) the enveloping spread of monopolistic central control.

EQUALITY

Innis was a liberal, and his view of the ideal society did not include socialistic egalitarianism; equality of opportunity and social mobility, on the other hand, clearly were central features. His primary concern was to promote the virtues of a society where monopoly power was checked through a balance between "contending hierarchies and competing media of communication." Innis's ideal society, one supposes, "would be one ruled by competing elites, each scouring society to find the most talented individuals in order to recruit and train them for social leadership" (Christian 1980, xii).

At the same time, Innis was highly sensitive to the arbitrary power, social inequality, and economic constraints imposed upon individuals on the margin, those who peopled peripheral nations or regions within international and national empires (whether formal or informal). Innis's perspective was informed by his own position as a colonial intellectual on the margins of an empire. His famous observation that Canada had made the journey "from colony to nation to colony" (Christian 1977, 28) encapsulates his belief that independent nationhood had not been an endpoint for Canada, but a temporary and transitory period between colonial status within first the French, followed by the British, then, finally, the American empire.

Innis's sensitivity to the inequality embedded within metropole-hinterland relations within empires was woven into his historical method. "He began from the perspective of the colonized. When he explored the underlying dynamics of economic and communication history, he did so by situating his analysis in detailed social histories of those peoples affected by major shifts in power and systems of control. His is without doubt an analysis from the hinterland" (Salter, 195). As noted above, his very "Canadianness" was central to his adoption of this vantage point, reinforced by his own "life and times" and his extensive travels to the more remote areas of Canada. His overseas service in World War I exposed him to the superior and high-handed treatment of Canadians and other "colonials" by the British political and military hierarchy. In the interwar period, he travelled extensively, canoeing two thousand miles down the Mackenzie River to the Arctic Ocean, visiting Yukon and the Klondike, northern Manitoba, and the western shores of Hudson's Bay, and travelling throughout northern Ontario, Quebec, the Maritimes, and the outports of Newfoundland. "From these travels Innis gained not only an unrivalled familiarity with the geography of Canada and a mastery of the technology of industries, but also a unique perspective on the impact of industrialism on Canada's north and other hinterland areas" (Berger, 87, 90).

Innis developed the concept of the "margin" to express the unequal relationship which developed in industrial society between economic and administrative centres and those hinterland regions from whence the centre drew usable resources. The margin existed in his work as "a space drawn into the axis of imperial economy, administration, and information that remains 'behind' (in temporal terms) or 'outside' (in terms of industrial or political power) ... its usable topographies are shaped, in dialectical interaction with its own resources, to serve the requirements of the empire" (Acland, 288). For the imperial metropole or "centre," the hinterland colony or "periphery" was primarily a possession, something to be used in a self-interested way. On the other hand, the periphery becomes dependent on the centre both as a market outlet for its resource commodities (staples) and also for a continual inflow of capital needed to pay for the industrial and transportation infrastructure of its resource-dependent development.

There were (and are) a number of distorting effects and negative consequences for the periphery that flow from the fundamentally unequal or "dependent" exchange relations that are established between centre and periphery. Periphery economies tend to be subject to instability and volatility (a "boom and bust" pattern of development) as exogenous forces set the agenda. Thus, the Canadian economy, primarily based on the "hewers of wood and drawers of water" model, lost many of the potential economic benefits from resource exploitation as these flowed abroad. Regions in Canada became overspecialized in certain types of resource production and burdened with high debt because of the transportation overheads required to ship resource wealth to foreign markets. This created the inherent risk of a growing disparity between the fixed costs of public indebtedness and the capacity of the economy to pay the increasingly high costs of resource development. Such conditions continually threatened to produce a virtual "staples trap" that posed a major obstacle to full national development. Staples-based development also exacerbated regional inequalities in Canada, as the national government sought to counter the negative effects of resource export dependence by using tariffs to force branch-plant industrial development in central Canada to service the national market. In this way the tariff, in Innis's opinion, became a racket for central Canada to keep what it had vis à vis the outlying regions (Drache, Introduction).

It should be noted, however, that Innis was not an anti-imperialist *tout court*. On the contrary, for Innis, balanced empires summed up what was best in human aspiration. Innis's concern was that particular forms of empire are more or less harmful, more or less destructive, to themselves as well as to their colonial possessions. This understanding of Innis's view of empires, and centre-margin relations more generally, helps to explain Innis's unmistakable rejection and excoriation of both American imperialism and Canadian nationalism. When Canada slipped irrevocably into the orbit of the American empire after World War II, its economy was pushed southwards in a continental direction and economic nation-building was put on the backburner. But the American empire was unlike the British; indeed, it was like no other, either preceding or contemporaneous. "It embodied the worst tendencies of the modern epoch, a radically imbalanced and unstable conglomeration altogether out of touch with the time dimension of culture and increasingly reliant on violence and mechanized knowledge to control space" (Whitaker, 828). To the extent that Canadian nationalism might provide the backbone for resistance to American control, it was viewed by Innis as a good thing, but only "insofar as it offered a creative alternative to this swollen Leviathan." If, on the other hand, Canadian nationalism did nothing more than reproduce internally what was worst in the imperial centre, then it merely serviced parochial and petty self-interests "that were equally as appalling as the imperial parent that gave it birth" (Whitaker, 828).

With increasing urgency, Innis warned that Canada was undergoing a process of re-colonization, this time by the United States, which, in the years after World War II, had become the centre for new international monopolies of knowledge and technology. This monopolization provided the basis for new conditions of colonization and new forms of empire that were not primarily military or administrative, but economic and ideological. Innis's concern was especially directed toward English Canada, and was fuelled by his fears about the effects of the "constant hammering" on Canada's cultural life of American commercialism (Acland, 250). Not only was this likely to destroy the potential for an independent and unique national culture in Canada, it was also likely to widen the gap between English and French-speaking Canadians. This led Innis, despite his suspicion of nationalism, to support the 1951 Massey Report's proposal of a strong, state-sponsored "public culture" in Canada (Acland, 251).

As noted, Innis's deep concern about the pervasive cultural and economic effects of Canada's reintegration into someone else's empire (the American) was explicitly tied to that new empire's imperial character and design, and most especially to the lack of cultural balance within it, a balance that Innis saw as crucial to a civilization's quality, stability, and durability. The same critical assessment, when applied to urban central Canada's relationship with its eastern, western and northern peripheries, informed Innis's growing skepticism and wariness about the centralizing and increasingly technocratic tendencies of Canadian nationalism. He warned against "social scientists carrying fuel to Ottawa to make the flames of nationalism burn more brightly" (Innis 1946, xii). This argument is congruent with the position adopted by Laurendeau, who called it "an abuse of language" to hear the centralizers called federalists, when in fact they were destroying the balance between governing powers that was at the heart of Confederation. Such warnings were also issued, for similar reasons, by Trudeau early in his career, and later for quite different reasons by George Grant.

Innis's conviction that the trend to centralism bode ill for Canada's eastern and western peripheries compelled him to urge provincial politicians to be vigilant in protecting and enhancing provincial autonomy in the face of centralizing forces in the 1930s and 1940s. These views on Innis's part were well-entrenched and never shaken, even when other English-Canadian intellectuals were rallying to the cause of a stronger federal government to deal with the Depression and the aftermath of the war. The reason for this is that Innis's analysis of the federal-provincial relationship was rooted in his exhaustive studies of the Canadian Pacific Railway, the fur trade, the cod fisheries, the mining and pulp and paper industries, and other forms of staples-based development that comprised the central core of Canadian economic history. This history clearly demonstrated for him the high cost imposed on the peripheries of centrally designed and centrally controlled economic development, in terms of economic volatility, distorted development, and social dislocation.

In Innis's estimation, the economic policies of the Canadian state had reinforced a pattern of development that benefited the centre to the detriment of the peripheries. So, when the economic ravages of the Depression years led others to call for the provinces to transfer many of their powers to Ottawa to allow the national government to deal with the crisis, Innis was one of the few Anglo-intellectual voices of dissent; when Keynesian policies of central economic management became all the rage, Innis resisted and protested; when political pressure on those provinces resisting postwar fiscal and political centralization became intense, Innis urged them not to relent (Creighton, 89; Berger, 101; Bickerton, 233–35). This support for a large measure of provincial autonomy, for a decentralized or, minimally, a balanced federation, and for changes to national policies to make them more regionally sensitive, reflects Innis's materialist analysis of the uneven regional distribution of benefits and costs associated with staples-based development in Canada. It also reflects his fundamental dislike for and distrust of centralizing bureaucrats and monopolistic concentrations of knowledge and power.

Innis's greatest empathy and concern, perhaps, was with those individuals, whether Aboriginal peoples, small farmers, fishers, woodsworkers, or miners and other industrial wage-earners, who were marginalized by economic and technological change. Innis's economic history delved into their key role in the staples economy, their conditions of work, their knowledge and skills, and the social dislocation they experienced with changes in trading patterns, technology, business cycles, industrial organization, resource depletion, or state policies. He was profoundly affected by the poverty and relative powerlessness of Depression-era Atlantic Canadian fishers which kept them "literally in a state of bondage ... destitute of the means of improvement ... doomed to perpetual servitude" (as quoted in Bickerton, 233). He greatly admired the courage, ingenuity, and dogged forbearance of fishers, and used the great injustice of their material circumstances to support his arguments for a revolution in the organization and prosecution of the fishing industry in order to address the evident power imbalances within it, including major changes in technique, export markets, jurisdiction, and government support for effective producer organizations (Bickerton, 233).

In a similar fashion, in his study of the fur trade, Innis stressed that "the Indian and his culture were fundamental to the growth of Canadian institutions" (as quoted in Drache, xlii), and that the abandonment of Aboriginal peoples, once the fur trade declined in economic importance, was a breach of the Crown's fiduciary responsibility, reflective of Canada's inability to transcend its colonial origins in order to build on its own traditions and accord full political rights to one of its founding peoples (Drache, xliii). Only toward the end of the twentieth century did the words and actions of Canadian governments and courts begin at last to lay the foundations of a new, post-colonial tradition of reconciliation with Aboriginal peoples, based on the constitutional entrenchment and legal protection of their unique status within Canada, and formal recognition that past governments had failed to acknowledge or protect their Aboriginal rights and deal honourably with the First Nations as equals.

COMMUNITY

In his study of the fur trade, Innis elucidated the materialist underpinnings of Confederation and the Canadian community. He provided an economic raison d'être for an independent, continent-spanning Canada, over and against the continentalist view that Confederation was an artificial creation that denied an otherwise "natural" north-south geography and economy. On the contrary, it was Innis's belief that "Canada developed not despite geography, but because of it" (Berger, 97). Its geographical coherence, its political unity, its various regional cultures, and its economic and social institutions were all bound together historically and continuously influenced by the country's staples-based economy and its place within a competitive international system of production and exchange (Berger, 95–9).

While Innis did not formally incorporate the concept of "community" into his thought, his attitude towards it was that of a certain kind of liberal, not of the utilitarian sort, but "one in tune with the tradition of civic republicanism" (Carey, 82). In his historical scholarship, Innis clearly shunned individualistic approaches to understanding perceptions and behaviour. Human perception and knowing were seen to be social rather than solitary activities. As an institutional economist, he was especially interested in the effect of social institutions on individual perception (Stamps, 57). As noted previously, Innis believed it was a society's institutions that created the conditions for individual freedoms, or alternatively for the suffocating restraint of monopoly and tyranny. To be more specific, Innis thought it was the historical evolution of a society's ensemble of social institutions that was responsible for creating the kind of community that could ensure a high quality of individual freedoms, in conjunction (necessarily) with political and economic stability. All these conditions were necessary for the full development of the individual talents and potentials within society.

Innis's collectivist orientation was centred in concern for the health and vitality of society perceived as an organic whole, and a recognition that the fate of the individual ultimately rested on the fate of his or her society. It was not, however, a collectivism that was explicitly or predominantly statist. The state was an institution that Innis fundamentally distrusted. This helps to explain why he consistently advocated a decentralized political system in Canada.

First and foremost, the centralization of power in Canada was opposed by Innis because he believed that all large concentrations of power (states included) "had self-destructive, empire-like qualities" (Stamps, 58). He thought it important to defend both the integrity and the diversity of provincial communities against centralizing and homogenizing forces – economic, technological, political – at the core of modern society. A "progressive community life" was crucial to a healthy, well-balanced, stable society, and this would be lost should local control over resources, economy, and the determination of community affairs be ceded to national (or global) decision-makers. To prevent or moderate this, to avoid becoming "storm centres to the modern international economy," provincial (as well as national) communities needed adequate institutional protections (Kroker, 1984, 82–3; Bickerton, 233–235; Drache, xvii).

Secondly, defending provincial autonomy was necessary to the maintenance of the traditions of responsible government in the provinces, a meaningful role for provincial legislatures, and the quality of local democracy. It also was congruent with Innis's concern to protect and shore up those few "time-biased" institutions in Canada that were still rooted in the oral tradition, a short list that included provincial legislatures. The operative principles of provincial legislatures were rooted in the oral tradition, which made them one of the few societal institutions in modern society that could conceivably act as a counterbalance to space-biased institutions such as the mass media, centralized bureaucracy, and the modern corporation, all of which were biased toward encompassing and exerting control over space.

As an "unrelenting materialist," Innis was profoundly aware that changes to the economic and technological base of a community would impact upon its politics, culture, and society. Nor was he mesmerized or enamoured with the "march of progress." He recognized that economic growth and development did not necessarily mean improvement. In fact, he warned that the rapid pace of change in modern society, if unchecked, had great destructive potential (Westfall, 39). Many communities, great and small, had throughout history become victims of economic and technological change. The historical interplay Innis posits between technologies of communication and the socio-political order suggests that the introduction of radically innovative technologies will have profoundly disruptive and often contradictory effects on the cultural and social fabric of civilizations: "on authority, power, values, public opinion, and intelligence ... world views collide, institutions are threatened, and cultures find themselves in crisis ... traditions, social mores, myths, and politics must fight for their lives" (Drache, xlviii).

Canada's fate as a national community was a source of great concern for Innis, and he was frankly pessimistic about the country's developmental trajectory. In his last years, he viewed the spread within Canadian society of rampant individualism, crass materialism, and pervasive present-mindedness with dark foreboding. He saw the source of this cultural change in the growing dominance of modern mass media, the insatiable expansion of the American commercial juggernaut, and the growing power and scope of a centralized state bureaucracy, all of which were monopolistic and biased toward social control over space. An additional concern for Innis was the seductive attraction of American-style abstract rights, legally guaranteed to individuals in a formal, written constitution. Innis preferred the more concrete liberties "that evolved over the course of a community's practical historical experience" and in a way "consistent with the continued life of the society" (Noble, 40).

Innis argued that these societal trends, which he attributed to Canada's willing if not eager absorption into the American empire, would bring about the progressive devaluation and deterioration of historical memory in Canada, the neglect of the common good, and ultimately the destruction of a distinctive culture and community (indeed, all sense of culture and community). Yet his calls for Canadians to resist American imperialism "in all its attractive guises" exhibited little faith that anything could be done and offered little by way of practical suggestions on how the slide (further into the American empire) might be reversed (Whitaker, 829).

CONCLUSION

Harold Innis was a groundbreaking and radically innovative thinker. With an academic career that spanned the 1920s, '30s, and '40s, he preceded the other thinkers discussed in this book by a generation or more. Whether in the subject matter he chose to study, the theories and methods he adapted and devised to do so, or the cultural values, sense of identity, and world outlook he brought to bear on this material, Innis was one of the first distinctively Canadian social scientists. His impact on Canadian politics during his lifetime, however, was for the most part indirect. Much more significant has been his intellectual legacy to thinkers in the social sciences who came after him, whether in economics, history, political science, or communications.

Innis's core concerns, which grew out of his extensive research into the political economy of staples development, were both quintessentially Canadian and eerily prescient of the events and issues associated with economic and political developments during the half-century after his passing. These concerns included the loss of Canadian identity and independence under the "hammer blows" of American commercialism; the threat to regional autonomy and self-governance from centralizing state bureaucrats; the key role of the university for a democratic society and the need to maintain its institutional autonomy from overweening political and corporate influence; the systemic social, economic, and political biases involved in the introduction of new technologies and modes of organization; and last but certainly not least the deleterious effects for individual freedom, cultural integrity, and societal stability of the tendency toward centralized, monopoly control over these new technologies (and the concentrated social power that attended such control).

As noted, these themes in Innis's researches and writings found reflection in the later work of many thinkers in many different disciplines. They are echoed, sometimes closely (as with Grant) in the perspectives offered by the other Canadian thinkers profiled in this book. Innis was clearly a forerunner and a path-breaker, and though his influence has seldom been direct, he did provide a broad framework of analysis, a direction of inquiry, and a research-cum-political agenda that helped to give both shape and substance to intellectual and political debates in this country.

CHAPTER THREE

Lament: The Anguished Conservatism of George Grant

George Grant (1918–1988) was one of English-speaking Canada's most celebrated and seminal twentieth-century thinkers. A professor of philosophy and religious studies at Dalhousie and McMaster universities from 1947 to 1984, Grant wrote and spoke forcefully and eloquently on a wide range of subjects, including history, religion, morality, ethics, technology, and of course, politics. Compared to the other thinkers discussed in this book, Grant's ideas about freedom, equality, and community are perhaps closest to those of Harold Innis (although Grant's critique of liberalism does share something in common with Charles Taylor). Indeed, Grant wrote approvingly about the intellectual contributions and path-breaking ideas of Innis, though he thought the political economist had not gone far enough in his critique of liberalism.

Like Innis, Grant was both critical of and skeptical about the role of universities in modern technological society. Unlike Innis, Grant was not a dominant presence in shaping the intellectual and academic milieu within which he toiled. For most of his career, he was an intellectual and academic maverick whose vision of the role of university teaching was overwhelmed and marginalized by the inexorable push toward highly specialized research as the core intellectual activity of university professors. Grant clearly saw Innis's earlier fears being realized: the university was rapidly becoming little more than a training institution whose role was to fulfill the workforce needs of a technological society. Yet there was little that Grant could do to prevent this change, other than to lament its coming to pass.

"Lament" features prominently in Grant's thinking, and the pessimism to be found in Innis's work is both more pronounced and more profound in Grant's. This gave his ideas a deep resonance with Canadians who were uneasy about the direction of postwar changes in Canadian culture and society. It also placed clear limits on the political and intellectual influence Grant could hope to wield within Canadian society, limits which Grant himself clearly understood. His reaction was to attempt to turn his own Department of Religion at McMaster into a subversive "fifth column" within the university. (Christian, 223) Grant recognized, however, that the economic, social, and political elite, as well as the great mass of the Canadian population, were fully committed to the kind of society that he railed against in his writings. This relegated him to the role of a respected but somewhat marginal intellectual voice, issuing siren-like warnings about economic and cultural developments, the main trajectory of which could not be reversed.

Grant was both a conservative and a nationalist, but a rather unorthodox one on both counts. His conservatism was of the classical, philosophical variety, rather than the contemporary version of free-market liberalism that now commonly passes for conservatism. Grant's classical conservatism was rooted in five basic dispositions: 1) a belief in divine purpose within history and God-given laws of morality; 2) maintenance of social order through restraint and respect for tradition; 3) a preference for variety rather than uniformity; 4) belief in a qualitatively good life, including the virtues of honour and duty; and 5) a belief that there are finite limits to human reason (Reimer, 54).

Grant was not critical of everything about modern liberalism, but he was adamantly opposed to what he understood to be its central premise or dominant assumption, namely, "that man is free to shape his life and the world in the way he desires" (Reimer, 51). This liberal understanding of freedom, and the place accorded to it as the essence of humanity, had created and sustained the relentless Western pursuit of domination over all nature, including human nature. Indeed, technological society was a natural and inevitable outcome of this liberal view of the cosmos and humanity's place within it.

Grant's conservatism was wedded to his Canadian nationalism. He despaired of the growing integration of Canadian and American societies and the consequent loss of a distinctive Canadian identity rooted in conservative values. Ironically, this led him to have a positive attitude toward socialist parties and movements, including the democratic left in Canada, especially during their heyday in the 1960s and 1970s. Grant's eventual disposition toward Canadian socialists, however, was that, like their liberal counterparts, they would inevitably lead Canadians down the path of a universally-administered, technology-driven, homogeneous society. Following the thought of Leo Strauss, Grant believed this future society would necessarily be a tyranny, one that would unhinge peoples the world over from all national customs and traditions, their character and lives instead to be determined by the needs of unbridled change and technological advance. This transformation would be heedless of the social cost in terms of ethics, morality, or any notion of "the good society."

In any event, Grant always believed the nationalist cause in the modern world to be a lost one, though he applauded and supported those willing to resist and struggle against inexorable forces they could not hope to defeat. At the same time, Grant's great pessimism about the future – which at times appeared nearly complete – was illuminated from within by a core of hope for humanity rooted in deep and unshakeable Christian faith. Grant was sure that Eternity awaited, and that this was not affected by the transitory historical outcomes of political and social processes here on earth. Moreover, nature itself could not be subdued forever; it would rebel and ultimately prevail over human arrogance. In the interim, Grant held to Sir Thomas More's famous dictum that, when all hope was lost of realizing "the good," it remained one's duty to act to prevent the very worst. It is in this context that Grant's philosophical and political interventions and remonstrations should be viewed.

EARLY AND LATER INFLUENCES

Grant's philosophical outlook and political ideas were shaped by his family life and early upbringing; by the political, cultural, and social environment of his intellectually formative years; and by the writings of several key philosophers. Grant was born into what one left-wing critic contemptuously dismissed as "a Fine Old Ontario

Family." In fact, Grant's forebears and relatives were very near, and in some cases at the very centre of, the Canadian Establishment: "the truest and bluest Toronto Loyalists" (Muggeridge, 47). One grandfather was Sir George Parkin, administrator of the Rhodes Scholarship, leading spokesman for Imperial Federation (by his own description a "wandering Evangelist of Empire"), and later headmaster of the exclusive Upper Canada College (Christian 1993, 8). Another grandfather, G.M. Grant, was widely known as Principal Grant for his long tenure as head of Queen's University (from 1877 until his death in 1902). He was no less influential as a fellow imperialist, "and no less ready to identify the progress of mankind with the spread of Anglo-Saxon civilization." (Taylor, 135) Grant's father William (who died when Grant was sixteen) also became headmaster of Upper Canada College. Grant's uncle was Vincent Massey, heir to the Massey-Harris farm machinery fortune, Canadian diplomat, and eventually Governor General. (This brings to mind the little ditty: "In Toronto there are no classes ... just the Masseys and the masses.")[1]

Growing up in this family milieu provided Grant with a strong sense of Canada's British heritage and connection, and the distinct values and world outlook on which Canada was based compared to its republican neighbour to the south. Grant's first book, published in 1945, lauded the imperial connection with Britain as a "third way" between American and Soviet empires. Indeed, Grant argued that an independent Canadian nationality depended on the maintenance and strengthening of the imperial connection. On the other hand, Grant – who was deeply religious from his boyhood onward – eventually reacted against certain elements of his upbringing, in particular the passionless, materialistic "secular protestantism" of his relatives. At the core of this sectarian worldview was an unquestioned commitment to "progress" as the central purpose of civilized existence. Grant spent most of his academic career thinking about the religious, social, and economic roots of this philosophical outlook, its long-term implications for humanity in general, and for Canadians in particular.

Naturally, Grant's early education was at Upper Canada College, from whence, not surprisingly, he progressed to Queen's University for his undergraduate studies. History was his passion, and he won the history medal in his senior year at Queen's. More important, he earned a Rhodes Scholarship which he took up at Balliol College,

Oxford, in the fall of 1939, just as the war was beginning. These war years in Britain were a period of emotional and intellectual turmoil for Grant, occasioning both personal crisis and revelation. He worked as an ambulance attendant and air raid warden in London during the Blitz, during which time he had a revelatory spiritual experience that deepened and extended his Christian beliefs. For the rest of his life Grant attempted to think through the meaning of his wartime "born again" experience, and "the truths to which it pointed" (Christian 1993, 86).

Psychological stress and deteriorating physical health forced Grant's early return to Canada in 1941. He resumed his Oxford studies at war's end in 1945, abandoning his initial academic objective of a law degree, pursuing instead the D. Phil. with a focus on theology and philosophy. His own explanation for the change was that "the war posed me with problems for which we needed an answer. That seems to me the beginning and end of philosophy" (as quoted in Christian 1993, 129). Grant's moral and philosophical views were shaped during these years by his encounter with the great thinkers, especially Plato. It was Plato who inspired Grant's belief in the idea of universal, eternal truths and the possibility, even necessity, of defining and pursuing "the good life." In 1947, despite having formally taken only one university-level philosophy course, Grant accepted a position in the philosophy department at Dalhousie University in Halifax, and before leaving England married Sheila Allen.

Grant's early university career was spent learning about academia and its politics, sometimes painfully. He was especially vulnerable to collegial scorn and criticism for his philosophical stance – Christian Platonism – which "was intimately bound up with belief in God" (Christian 1993, 161). Also during these years Grant was acquainting himself more thoroughly and deeply with Plato. He thought Plato's *Republic* was the most influential book other than the Bible for the Western world because of its key teaching that justice was what measured and defined us as human beings (Christian 1993, 211).[2]

In 1950, Grant obtained his "formal qualifications" for the career of university professor by submitting his dissertation on the Scottish liberal theologian John Oman to his Oxford examiners. Though rarely explicity referred to later in his life, the thesis contained four broad themes that would form continuing threads in his philosophical thought.

First, that modern science had cut humanity off from nature and hence the possibility of approaching the divine through nature. Second, the success of modern science is, in some important way, linked to Calvinism and its emphasis on will. Third, the preoccupation with free will as the fundamental characteristic of human beings has weakened the grounding for human moral equality, which depends on man's relationship to God. Finally, the true test of any philosophy is its capacity to give moral guidance during a crisis. (Christian 1993, 149)

As Grant once noted, "the worst tragedies will occur where great responsibility operates in metaphysical confusion" (169).

Grant's academic career changed course at the end of the 1950s. A series of radio lectures for CBC in 1958 entitled "Philosophy in the Mass Age," published the following year, "established Grant's reputation among academics across the country as a dynamic, original and powerful thinker" (Christian 1993, 192). Grant left Dalhousie,[3] and after a false start with Toronto's newly established York University in 1959 that left him briefly unemployed, joined the new Department of Religion at McMaster University in Hamilton, Ontario.[4]

In the 1960s, Grant's intellectual as well as practical involvement in Canadian politics deepened. His family had close historical as well as personal ties with the Progressive Conservative party, and Grant's own belief in an unchanging moral law would naturally lead to a conservative political stance, "since conservatism understands the truth of order and limit, both in social and personal life" (191). Yet modern conservatism, in Grant's view, had become "little more than the justification of the continuing rule of the businessman and the right of the greedy to turn all activities into sources of personal gain" (191). Instead, Grant accepted an invitation from Michael Oliver to join a group of left-wing intellectuals (including Pierre Trudeau) in producing a 1961 collection of essays entitled *Social Purpose for Canada*, aimed at helping to create a new party that would be allied with the labour movement. The invitation was perhaps not so odd when one considers that Grant's *Philosophy in the Mass Age* had spoken kindly of Marx and was radically critical of modern capitalism. Grant's collaboration in this project produced an essay that "proposed an ethic of community as an alternative to the ethic that drove state capitalist mass society."[5]

It was the tumultuous political events in Canada in 1963 that brought Grant fully and irrevocably into the Canadian political debate, and made him a national figure. The demise of the minority Diefenbaker government in a hail of accusations and intrigue stimulated Grant to produce what would become his most widely read and influential piece of political analysis and commentary. The political crisis, provoked by the Canadian government's refusal to adopt the American nuclear arsenal, both at home and abroad, led to the parliamentary defeat of Diefenbaker's Progressive Conservatives by the combined votes of the Liberal, NDP, and Social Credit opposition.[6] Grant's desire to write an article explaining what he saw as the deeper meaning of these political events turned into his celebrated book *Lament for a Nation*.

While *Lament* has often been interpreted as a pro-Diefenbaker book and a "call-to-arms" for Canadian nationalists, Grant himself disavowed this. Grant recognized that Diefenbaker was a prairie populist who often mistook rhetoric for policy, and whose "small-town free enterprise ideology was 'entirely inadequate' to comes to terms with the society that had arisen in Central Canada since the war." Moreover, Diefenbaker was unwilling to recognize the rights of French Canadians as a community (Christian 1993, 247). However, his many failings as catalogued by Grant – his massive egotism, his messianism without content, his appalling choice of French Canadian colleagues – were counterbalanced by certain redeeming virtues: a fundamental belief in freedom within the law, social egalitarianism, and most especially, loyalty and patriotism (Christian and Grant 1998, 135).

"[Diefenbaker's] nationalism was old-fashioned, out-of-date in the technological age; but his courage was admirable and, 'whatever else he might have been, he was not false'" (Christian 1993, 265). This unabashed nationalism especially struck a chord with Grant because it recognized that to be independent Canada must maintain its strong connections to Britain; the only alternative was the embrace of the United States and an end to Canadian distinctiveness. In Grant's opinion, what tipped the scales in the latter direction, and away from a fading Canadian nationalism, "was that the large corporations, where real power lay, knew nothing of loyalty, only interest. That directed them south" (Christian 1993, 248). As Grant saw it, corporate interests required that Diefenbaker's government be sacrificed on the altar of continentalism.

The main point of this political episode for Grant was that nothing could stop the expansion of American-style technological capitalism and its accompanying ideology of progress. Canadians themselves were deeply implicated in this takeover. Far from resisting it, they fundamentally (if not always consciously) desired it.

> Over the years the independence of Canada had been continually eroded, not so much by the external actions of the Americans, as by the increasing acceptance of the attractiveness of the American vision of modernity ... Conservatives could delay, but they could not prevent its triumph; they would fail because, in their hearts, they too thought it was right ... The Liberal party's accomplishment was that it managed [this process] with a minimum of fuss ... They made people comfortable with necessity (Christian 1993, 249–50).

For those who thought Grant was trying to provoke a nationalist response with his book, Grant's reply was that he was talking about the end of Canadian nationalism, not its revival. His was a lament for the end of Canada as a sovereign and distinct nation, an end which in his mind had already irrevocably come to pass. "I was saying that this is over and people read it as if I was making an appeal for Canadian nationalism. I think that is just nonsense. I think they just read it wrongly" (as quoted in Christian, 251). Canadians might be better off to slow the process of continental integration, because in Grant's opinion even residual nationhood was better than none. But, "formal annexation by the United States would eventually come, and when it did it would have only a minor impact" (Christian 1993, 250).

So Canada, according to Grant, was fated to disappear into the voracious maw of technology-worshipping American liberalism. Still, despite its profound pessimism on this count, *Lament for a Nation* became one of the most widely read and influential books on Canadian politics, making a central contribution to the revival of Canadian nationalism. *Lament* was both invigorating and uplifting for a variety of individuals and groups of many political stripes: social movement and community activists, nationalists and ecologists, socialists and conservatives. It helped to shape the country's politics for more than two decades, culminating in the great free trade debate of 1988 and its political and economic aftermath. What accounts for this apparent paradox? It perhaps resides in the fact that at the core of Grant's analysis is a prescription for human action: that humans should live with courage in the face of inexorable technological forces; that they should do what they can to limit its tyranny and preserve human freedom and dignity, the potential for which is realizable only within well-ordered and cohesive communities (Christian and Grant 1998, 99–101).

While Grant would subsequently publish other influential and powerfully argued books that expanded and developed his political ideas, notably *Technology and Empire* (1969), *English-Speaking Justice* (1974), and *Technology and Justice* (1986), it would be *Lament* that would imprint itself on the Canadian psyche and stimulate wide-ranging discussion and debate around the issue of Canadian identity and autonomy in the second half of the twentieth century.

FREEDOM

An assessment of Grant's œuvre by his biographer William Christian suggests that one pole of Grant's thought was his Christianity and his abiding faith in the transcendent and eternal; the other his interest in the phenomenon of freedom, which had become central in the Western world. Never before in history had human beings defined and understood themselves primarily as free. Attempting to reconcile human freedom, conceived as the power to order the world according to human preference, and a transcendent and determining moral order by which human actions can be judged became Grant's philosophic life's work. This meant illuminating the meaning of freedom in the West and understanding why it commanded such respect (Christian 1993, 177).

At the centre of Grant's political and social analysis was his great trepidation that Canadian society (along with the whole of Western civilization) was headed towards a universal, homogeneous state that would sharply circumscribe human freedom. It was the intellectual influence of philosopher Leo Strauss – from whom Grant learned more than from "any other contemporary writer" (Christian 1993, 226) – that convinced Grant that this future society would be "radically destructive of humanity" (Christian 1993, 224). Two other thinkers, the philosopher Alexandre Kojeve and the French sociologist Jacques Ellul, gave Grant a fuller understanding of the dynamics of the modern world: where technological society was headed, and "the unity behind many individual manifestations of modern technology and how its spirit permeated every aspect of contemporary life" (Christian 1993, 227).

It's not that Grant didn't understand or appreciate the modern political liberties enjoyed by people in Western liberal democratic society; Grant acknowledged that such liberties constituted "a central human good." He believed these traditional liberties, however, to be threatened by the concentration of technology on mastery over nature and human beings. As Grant noted, for centuries the energies of Western society had been directed toward this, with the motive that by it, people should be free. "Freedom was the rallying cry." Advancing technology became the means to attain this freedom, while freedom itself – conceived as the freedom to change any order that stood in the way of "progress" (itself understood as technological advance) – became essential to the development and introduction of new technologies. The most fertile soil for this new set of beliefs was North America, the only society that had no history of its own before the age of progress, and therefore no restraining traditions.[7]

In this sense, the onset of technological civilization and the freedom granted by modern contractual liberalism were intimately linked. Both had their roots in elements of thought peculiar to Western Christianity, and more particularly the strand of Christianity that can be referred to as "secularized Protestantism." Grant thought this had come about because a key element of early Protestantism was faith in providence – the progressive movement of the world toward the Kingdom of God. However, as belief in God diminished in the West under the assaults of Enlightenment thinkers and the scientific revolution, faith in providence was transformed into a popular belief in progress. As a corollary, "Science and Technology" replaced God as the means of redemption. What bothered Grant most about this was the "total freedom" which technological liberalism gave to modern people. Grant's conservatism led him naturally to resist this notion of freedom without limits.

Grant's answer to limitless freedom was to "assert the existence of a moral law which limits man's freedom," rooted in the idea of God. Without this belief in God, there was no theoretical limit to freedom, therefore no practical limit, "making any action permissible" (Taylor 1982, 143). This has led to the erosion of individual and social morality. It has done this by making individual will supreme over truth, beauty, goodness, or any other substantive value that can be traced to non-rational origins in tradition, religion, belief in a supreme being, or a sense of an eternal order that is beyond human control or understanding. Ultimately, this "triumph of the will" supercedes all other social or moral considerations, leading directly to the assertion of individual choice and rights as the "prime directive" for liberal society. This "will to technology" cannot be separated from liberal society's discourse on freedom. Western technological civilization grants people the freedom to create values in the pursuit of the greatest happiness of the greatest number through capitalist technology. For Grant, legalized abortion and other issues associated with advances in reproductive technologies was illustrative of this.[8]

Grant's understanding of freedom is certainly at variance with that offered by modern liberalism. He believes the first obligation of humans as citizens is to be free, but by "free" he means the capacity "to do what is right," not "to do as we like" (Cooper, 28). Freedom comes from "knowing the truth of things" rather than gaining mastery over human beings and nature. "In the long pull freedom without the knowledge of reality is empty and vacuous" (Taylor 1982, 89). Clearly, the knowledge of reality provided by science and technology is not the "truth of things" that Grant has in mind. In this sense, Grant's notion of freedom, much like Charles Taylor's, has a moral dimension. Both believe that the "goodness" of the choices made by individuals can be judged, and that not all choices made by individuals are equivalent, either in terms of their manifestation of or their contribution to human freedom.

In another sense as well, Grant is similar to Taylor, Innis, and other thinkers in this book, in that he understood freedom to be primarily a social good, something that is possible only in a certain kind of society, with certain kinds of institutions that preserve the conditions for freedom. Freedom becomes possible in the context of a social order that embodies and respects social stability and the rule of law. This, Grant argued, was at the heart of the Canadian conservative tradition: "that freedom should neither endanger the freedom of others nor disrupt the pattern of social order … [Canadians] revealed this in their respect for law and authority, in an educational system rooted in the strict disciplines and in their adherence to sane and orthodox religions rooted in the past" (Grant as quoted in Christian 1993, 108).

Grant and Taylor are not in accord on everything, however. While both are distinctively Canadian thinkers, and both study modernity in terms of animating notions of the good, in at least one important respect Grant's conception of technology leads him to a different interpretation of the modern condition from Taylor. As we have seen, Grant believes that the hegemony of an epistemological stance in the modern world which objectifies the universe, therefore permitting human control of that universe through technical mastery, has led to the rise of an industrial and organizational apparatus – the technological society – which ultimately corrodes the very liberal values which made possible its ascendancy. In turn this leads to the gradual replacement of public freedom with a "soft despotism" of bureaucratized technology (Millard and Forsey, 10).

Not that Grant, like Taylor, isn't keenly aware of technology's benefits, particularly its benevolent and egalitarian role in "relieving the condition of man." Grant asserts that technology serves the ideal of "building a society of free and equal men by the overcoming of chance" (Grant 1969a, 138). But Grant also understands that technology "intrinsically, is nourished by an ideal of mastery in its own right ... The 'technological dynamo' has grown increasingly divorced from its concern with human welfare, moving toward a self-perpetuating 'mastery of the planet' unmotivated by prior goods" (Millard and Forsey, 15). "Changing the world becomes ... ever more an end in itself," argues Grant. "We will, not so much for some end beyond will, but for the sake of the willing itself ... Our freedom can even start to make over our own species" (Grant 1969b, 19). For Grant, then, mastery is an inherent part of the technological enterprise. "As moderns are bound up in technology, so they are in the will-to-mastery" (Millard and Forsey, 20).

This means that unlike Taylor, Grant foresees not only the possibility but the increasing likelihood of an amoral modernity. "Amoral agency" is an option "that grows more irresistible as the technological dynamo marches on, producing human subjects who have fully internalized that deconstruction of morality which is innate in the project" (Millard and Forsey, 21). This is a much more pressing worry for Grant than for Taylor, and lies at the core of his great pessimism and foreboding about the future.

EQUALITY

Grant's family history and his elitist educational background – from Upper Canada College to Queen's University to Oxford – does not suggest that he had much personal exposure to the lives of the less advantaged. Nor is conservatism, the political and philosophical tradition with which Grant identified, generally viewed as particularly concerned with promoting equality – indeed, quite the opposite. But here Grant's rather unorthodox conservatism reveals itself. While he did acknowledge "the conservative principle of hierarchy – which arises from a diversity of talents," he argued that "this must be balanced against the principle of equality – which arises from the absolute worth of all men" (Taylor 1982, 145).

During his lifetime, Grant was viewed for the most part as a friend and fellow-traveller by the Canadian political left. This was due both to his scathing critique of Western capitalist society (with its dominant passions – materialism and greed) and to his nationalist "call to arms" against Canada's absorption into the American empire. In Grant's view, some measure of socialist planning wedded to nationalism was necessary in order to restrain the liberal drive to continentalism and thereby absorption into the American empire. "What is socialism," Grant asked, "if not the use of government to restrain private greed in the name of social good?" (1965, 59) In these circumstances, Canadian conservatives were "Red Tories" or they were nothing. Grant himself was regarded by many as the epitome of the Red Tory: a conservative who viewed Canadian socialism as a variant of conservatism (rather than the "liberals in a hurry" that long-time Liberal prime minister Mackenzie King believed them to be).

Grant's ideas about equality had neither liberal nor socialist roots. Whereas liberals tended to emphasize an individual's right to equality of opportunity, and socialists the need for government to address the perverse and arbitrary effects of economic inequality in a capitalist society, Grant argued that the equality of all human beings was fundamentally a question of their equal moral worth. It was Grant's religious beliefs that provided the philosophical foundation for his view of equality. Individuals, regardless of their abilities, were human beings who possessed a soul. This made them equal before God. This in turn made it incumbent upon the state to treat each person as important; to grant each individual the legal and social status of an equal; and to craft and preserve a just society that reflected this basic truth. Arrayed against this fundamental equality, differences in individual talents were, Grant thought, a relatively petty consideration. (Christian and Grant 1988, 69–70)

In "An Ethic of Community," Grant made two further points about economic and social equality in modern society. First, it was now possible for the majority to possess large amounts of goods with a high degree of leisure. Equality of participation in this leisure will become an increasingly pressing necessity for society's economic and social health. Secondly, the form of human existence created by mass technological society makes imperative a struggle for "equality of participation in mind." Broad accessibility to higher education is therefore a fundamental characteristic of a just and egalitarian society.[9] However, Grant came to believe that the realization of these opportunities for greater equality, which if acted upon would constitute a major attack on social injustice, were blocked by the capitalist ethic (Taylor 1982, 145). Only by adopting "a clearly defined ethic of community which understands the dignity of every person and is determined on ways of fulfilling that dignity" would society's new potential for greater equality and justice be fully realized. (Christian and Grant 1988, 75)

Despite all this, it could be argued that a concern with equality was not at the heart of Grant's political analysis. Indeed, furthering individual equality might be seen as one of the central principles underlying the global push toward the universal, homogeneous, technological state that Grant so adamantly opposed. That he was concerned with equality can be explained by his view that the new technological society would radically diminish (if not erase) both human individuality and the diversity of nations. "Where modern science has achieved its mastery, there is no place for local cultures" (as quoted in Taylor 1982, 146). He used all his intellectual and polemical skills to warn against and denounce these impending losses, in terms of individual freedom, cultural diversity, and national distinctiveness.

It was with regard to the central importance of preserving the diversity of national cultures that Grant converged in his views with French Canadian thinkers such as Laurendeau and Rioux. Grant was a conservative convinced of the inherent value and culture-bearing qualities of whole, organic societies. This necessarily made him a Canadian nationalist intent upon resisting the cultural domination of the American hegemon. Grant, then, was acutely sensitive to the threat of assimilation faced by both English and French Canada. Like Laurendeau, he initially viewed the alliance of the two Canadas (English and French) as critical to the survival of both, but especially Canada's indigenous English-speaking society. However, as he became increasingly pessimistic about English Canada's capacity to define itself, or to protect itself as a nation against the threat of cultural assimilation, he worried that Canada's English-speaking culture was little more than a Trojan horse for the American cultural monolith. Quebec nationalists, he mused, might be better served to resist the embrace of English-speaking Canada and concentrate on their own cultural survival (Christian and Grant 1988, 107). In any event, he thought the greatest obligation of all Canadians was to resist assimilation, "to work for a country which is not simply a satellite of any empire" (Christian and Grant 1988, 90).

Such demonstrations of solace and support for the nationalist project in Quebec did not alter Grant's opinion that French Canadians ultimately would fail to resist the pull of continentalism. The reason was simple. Quebec nationalism could only assert itself successfully by an identification with technological advance; technological advance entailed disappearance of indigenous differences that gave substance to nationalism. In other words, while Quebec nationalists might eventually succeed in their political sovereignty project, Quebec society inevitably would be stripped of its unique content: its cultural differences (Taylor 1982, 147). Both English- and French-speaking Canadians were fated to lose the distinct traditions and values that act as a barrier to the homogenizing rationality of technological modernity; both would be blended into an American-centred melting pot of cultural sameness. Greater equality for individuals might well be one of the outcomes of this process, but at the cost of enormous cultural losses.

COMMUNITY

Community was at the core of Grant's political thought. A profound sense of the historical difference between his own English Canadian community and the American community to the south motivated and informed many of his ideas and much of what he wrote. Grant's desire to preserve the distinctive values and characteristics of his community, as he saw them, even as he witnessed the gradual but sure transformation of that community in the post-war era, provided the tension and the spark in his political thought. It was also a principal source of his great pessimism. Conservatism,

Grant argued, was the set of principles which embodied and guided the Canadian way. It enriched Canadian democracy "because it understood better [than did American democracy] the dependence of freedom upon the law." (Christian and Grant 1998, 136) Yet genuine conservatism, Grant acknowledged, was impossible in an era wedded to both the spirit and the material benefits of technological progress. Therefore, Canada, at least the Canada that Grant cherished, was fated to disappear as surely as snow melting in spring. Grant's nationalism, like Diefenbaker's, was not feasible in a technological era. "The impossibility of conservatism in our era is the impossibility of Canada" (1965, 68).

The Canadian community whose passing Grant lamented was clearly one which was British in its heritage and traditions. If Diefenbaker was the last prominent politician to unequivocally express his affection for and attachment to a Canadian identity that was intimately linked to British institutions and values, then Grant was the last prominent political thinker to do so. Grant's attachment to and preference for what he recognized to be a vanishing Canadian identity and culture was also a function of his sense that Canada was still a country in which citizenship meant something more than it did in the United States of America. "Traditional democratic means – the vote and support for political parties – have more meaning in our smaller sphere. Political choice is both more real and more possible in Canada." (Christian and Grant 1988, 85)

Grant was not merely being nostalgic, however, when he lamented the disappearance of Canada's indigenous traditions. He lamented the passing of all indigenous traditions, including his own, because "it is only through some particular roots, however partial, that human beings first grasp what is good and it is the juice of such roots which for most men sustain their partaking in a more universal good" (as quoted in Taylor 1982, 152). For Grant the erosion of Canadian sovereignty,

> although fated, was a matter of genuine loss, something to be lamented ... [because] people first encountered the good not absolutely, but in things that were their own, their friends, locality, traditions, country, or civilization. To reach God it was necessary to pass beyond this love, but also to pass through it. (Christian 1993, 263–4)

The importance of retaining community and national traditions is primary for Grant, "the best basis for the practical life." Indeed, when he wrote his *Lament for a Nation*, his arguments were based more on tradition (the loss thereof) than philosophy. "Those who loved the older tradition of Canada may be allowed to lament what has been lost, even though they do not know whether or not that loss will lead to some greater political good" (Christian and Grant 1988, 83). This reverence for tradition made him somewhat scornful towards those ideologues who embraced liberalism as converts, out of rejection of their own particular traditions. In Grant's opinion, their liberalism tended to be unbalanced and unchecked by the pragmatism gained from lived experience with the imperfect workings of liberal institutions. Pierre Trudeau was just such a figure in Grant's eyes: the archetypal modern technocrat, a formidable politician who embraced the universalist appeal of liberalism because of his own visceral distaste for and rejection of the French Canadian tradition. Grant saw Trudeau's appeals to universalism as fostering the economic and social integration of Canadians, as individuals and as a country, into the whole Western system. This meant integration into a smoothly functioning continental system and the eventual submersion of any distinctive Canadian identity or values (Christian 1993, 340–41; Christian and Grant 1988, 104).

Like the other writers discussed in this book, with the possible exception of Trudeau, Grant understood community to be essential to the development of the identity, personality, and values of the individual. Learning how to live with others in a community, how to contribute to its maintenance and healthy functioning – in effect, how to help that community to socially cohere – was one of the fundamental purposes of a human being's existence.[10] Human freedom is possible only in the context of a social order and community undergirded by tradition, providing both limits and supports for that freedom. "When men have no easily apprehensible 'law of life' given them by tradition, the danger is that their freedom will be governed by an arbitrary and external law of mediocrity and violence which will debase their humanity rather than fulfill it" (Christian and Grant 1988, 61).

The universal, homogeneous, technological society which Grant sees unfolding will constitute a tyranny because it will be a society in which "community" is dessicated, where secular state and capitalist corporation continually reorganize and restructure society in accordance with the capitalist ethic and the needs of technology. Rationality, efficiency, and convenience are the ordering principles; tradition, custom, fraternity, and the social bonds of community are devalued and displaced. The need to reconcile individual freedom with the good of the community is ignored, and the scope and possibility for human freedom and dignity shrink accordingly.

> What can be done to make our cities communities in which the human spirit can flourish? ... How can we cultivate freedom for the individual without having it become identified (as it is now) with ruthless self-interest and the grasping of more than a fair share? ... A society is not likely to be a place of healthy loyalties and ordered cohesion if its members are taught to pursue first and foremost their economic self-interest and if its leaders are chosen from those who pursue that self-interest more ruthlessly. (Christian and Grant 1988, 63–64)

Like Innis and Laurendeau, Grant became increasingly critical and suspicious of the post-war trend toward political centralization. Though initially he supported this development as a means to maintain Canadian independence, once he became convinced that the country was lost to American domination, "he favoured decentralization as a way to retard the process of homogenization" (Christian 1993, 340). Grant thought regions outside Ontario which had not yet fully embraced Americanization might find ways to defend their integrity as communities. Besides, at the national level no real political option remained. By the 1970s all three national parties (Liberals, Conservatives, New Democrats) had given up the nationalist cause by shedding those factions or individuals who seriously challenged continentalist logic. "The three Canadian parties have destroyed their nationalist wings: the squashing of Walter Gordon by Lester Pearson when the former annoyed the business community; the removal of the Waffle from the NDP when it angered the unions; the destruction of Diefenbaker and his followers by Camp and the business Tories" (Christian and Grant 1988, 152).

Still, even if Grant felt the final outcome was preordained, he believed in the virtue and worth of resistance to universalizing and homogenizing forces. "It is surely a nobler stance to go down with all guns blazing than to be acquiescently led, whether sadly or gladly, into the ever greater homogenizing of our country into the American mass" (Christian and Grant 1988, 153). There was an inherent value in fighting to maintain some measure of individual and societal autonomy, to minimize to the greatest extent possible

American cultural, economic and political influence over Canada. This was true even if, ultimately, the dynamic technological modernity that was the spearhead of this American influence was fated to encompass the globe. Besides, the option of simply accepting one's fate and ceasing to resist by retreating from the world – "dreaming the anti-social dream" as Grant called it – was not for him a real alternative. "Man is by nature a social being, therefore it is a kind of self-castration to try to opt-out of the society one is in ... We cannot opt for that mysticism which tries to reach the ultimate joy by bypassing our immediate relations and responsibilities in the world" (Christian and Grant 1988, 100).

CONCLUSION

George Grant, like each of the other five thinkers here, was strongly influenced in his thought by his own personal and family history, as well as the social and political milieu that surrounded him. His ideas and arguments were shaped by his family traditions and beliefs, as well as his strong attachment to the idea and the substance of a distinctive Canadian identity rooted in a particular historical experience and set of values that differed significantly from the experience and values of the United States. Grant's own articulation of this Canadian identity and ethic cast him as the quintessential 'Red Tory': an amalgam of traditional Canadian conservatism, stubborn nationalism, and a suspicion of capitalism that made some measure of socialist planning palatable if not desireable.

Grant's influence on Canadian politics as a public intellectual far outstrips his academic contribution to philosophy. His political appeal was in part attributable to this cross-partisan ideological appeal. A greater measure of it, however, can be explained by his eloquent advocacy of resistance and struggle in the face of seemingly inexorable forces. Grant's great pessimism about the future of Canada, and indeed the whole of human civilization notwithstanding, he managed to stir the imagination and steel the determination of nationalists, socialists, communitarians, ecologists, student activists, and all manner of Canadians who shared his premonitions about the long-term implications of the dominant ideology of technological liberalism and the kind of society it was fostering. In this important sense, Grant seems the natural inheritor and extension of an important part of Harold Innis's intellectual legacy, though a much more public and dramatic expositor of that legacy than ever was Innis.

In a quite different sense, Grant is more akin to (and at home with) fellow philosopher Charles Taylor, both in terms of the sources of his thought as well as his manner of presenting and explicating it. The influence of the ancients on Grant's thought, especially Plato, is clear, as are the arguments and insights of later philosophers such as Kant, Marx, Nietzsche, and most directly Strauss, as well as the French sociologist Jacques Ellul. A quite separate yet searing influence is Grant's fervent Christianity, something which clearly distinguishes him from both Innis and Taylor. All these elements and influences were at play in Grant's thought, combining to create an eloquent and profound, sometimes outrageous, and most definitely unique Canadian thinker.

CHAPTER FOUR

André Laurendeau: The Search for Political Equality and Social Justice

André Laurendeau is surely the intellectual who had the greatest impact on French Canadian, and later Québécois, political thinking about equality. More than any other thinker discussed in this book, his ideas were in harmony with the political realities of his time. Much of Laurendeau's post-World War II thought has been popularised and is still frequently cited as forming the backbone for a political solution to the Quebec/Canada impasse.[1]

Laurendeau played an active role in several groups during his life. In 1932, at the age of twenty, he co-founded the *Jeune-Canada* movement with, among others, Pierre Dansereau, who became its president, Lucien L'Allier, and Gérard Filion. Its founding members were active participants in the Cercle Crémazie, a literary group that met at the Collège Sainte-Marie (Dansereau, 1990, 180–1).

The Jeune-Canada movement was initially characterized by its xenophobia. Although it was not anti-immigrant, the "old stock" French culture was to be emulated. At the time, the role of the Church was considered essential to the survival and strengthening of the French-Canadian culture in North America (Anctil 1990, 231).

At an early phase in his public life one finds expressions of anti-Semitism in Laurendeau's thinking. For example, he delivered an anti-Semitic speech during a meeting of Jeune-Canada in April 1933 (Anctil 1988, 112–13). The influence exercised by Abbé Lionel

Groulx on Laurendeau at that time is clear. Groulx and Arthur Laurendeau, André's father, pursued many common objectives as demonstrated by their involvement in the *Action française*, and later in their founding of the *Action nationale* in 1933, five years after the former went bankrupt.

In 1934, Laurendeau defended the relationship between nationalism and Catholicism while editor-in-chief of *Le Semeur*, the journal of the Catholic Association of French-Canadian Youth. He left *Le Semeur* and the Jeune-Canada movement the following year to study in France.

It was during his time in France that Laurendeau's position on nationalism changed. He saw firsthand the atrocities committed against Jews in Europe and the intolerance that could be associated with nationalism. His time in Paris from 1935 to 1937 while attending lectures from some of France's leading intellectuals at the Sorbonne, the Collège de France, and the Catholic Institute represent a turning point in the evolution of his political thought. The "ravissement parisien"[2] had many repercussions on the political thought of Laurendeau, the most important of which was to link nationalism with the liberal ideas and social concerns that increasingly shaped his worldview. His principal mission upon his return to Quebec was to emphasize the relationship between the national and social dimensions of French-Canada's situation, an interpretation that was later called "neo-nationalism."

In a letter sent to Abbé Groulx in 1936, one can sense that Laurendeau no longer accepted the prevailing leadership in Quebec. He wrote: "I met some new men and some new groups, from Catholic teachers to Marxist writers. At least this helps to broaden my perspective. I am trying to open myself to all the influences that appear to be good, even though there may be some risk involved ... the more I look around me, the more I realise our lack of intellectual daring" (quoted in Horton 1992, 47).

Laurendeau was not comfortable with the idea of accepting established dogmas; he preferred to see ideas challenged. His encounters with French intellectuals, always questioning the status quo and demanding a fairer economic system, had a major impact on him. According to Denis Monière, "He realised that an intensified search for spiritual values could move in tandem with the movement for economic change and social progress. Not only did he become more conscious of social questions, he also brought back with him some radically anti-capitalist ideas" (Monière 1983, 100, our translation). This critical view of capitalism and its excesses was present throughout his life. It probably explains the sympathy he later harboured toward the young intellectuals behind the radical left journal, *Parti Pris*, whose actions he interpreted as manifestations of their vision to change the world and create an egalitarian society (Dion 1993, 190).

During his intellectually formative years in Paris Laurendeau explored the progressive political writings of influential authors such as Jacques Maritain, Thierry Maulnier, Emmanuel Mounier, Nicolai Berdyayev, Daniel Rops, and Étienne Gilson. Influenced by the Catholic French journal *L'Esprit*, Laurendeau condemned Franco's Insurrectionists in the Spanish Civil War and saw their actions as being driven by capitalist, fascist, and feudal-clerical interests (Behiels 1985, 27). In March 1936 he wrote to his parents that,

> Since my arrival in Europe, my admiration for the work of Mussolini, Hitler and even Salazar has diminished ... Have I the right to forget that Italian nationalism curiously threatens world peace? ... Must I forget that in the land of Italian nationalism personal freedom hardly exists anymore? Or that the labour movement has been checked, and that certain historical advantages that had been won only at great sacrifice are now lost indefinitely? Have I the right to forget the grave danger that Catholic-fascist cohabitation represents for the Church? (Reproduced in Monière 1983, 88, our translation).

Laurendeau was of the view that "one could love one's country without adhering to totalitarian ideologies." This critique of extremism did not lead him, however, to an uncritical embrace of liberalism as the antidote of fascism. Laurendeau understood that liberalism protects the freedom of high finance and of trusts, which he found equally repugnant. He adhered neither to communism nor to fascism nor to capitalism (Monière 1983, 112). Monière adds that Laurendeau "believed that nationalism had to distance itself from conservative influences, [though] he was uncertain as to what social content it had to possess. The idea of social and political vision remains an open question in Laurendeau, who tried to give nationalism a very personal foundation" (Monière 1983, 112, our translation).

When Laurendeau returned to Montreal in 1937 to replace his father at the head of *L'Action nationale*, he distanced himself from his friends still active in Jeune-Canada, particularly those who were supporting the Union Nationale premier of Quebec, Maurice Duplessis (Guillaume 1990, 124). Moreover, Laurendeau strove to dissociate nationalism from right-wing political thought. Monière writes: "He was convinced that nationalism and conservatism do not necessarily go hand in hand. In his opinion, a modern nationalism must accept social change and be open to the world" (1990, 193, our translation). Laurendeau began the task of rejuvenating nationalist principles when he started writing for the *L'Action nationale* and, a decade later, for the daily newspaper *Le Devoir*.

The Conscription Crisis of 1942 constitutes an important moment in Laurendeau's life, as it led him into the political arena.[3] The plebiscite of 1942 was designed to release the federal government from its commitment not to impose conscription for overseas service, a promise that had been firmly made during the 1940 federal election that saw Quebec swept by Mackenzie King's Liberals. In reaction to the plebiscite, provincial autonomists rallied around the Ligue pour la défense du Canada which gave birth to a new political movement, the Bloc populaire canadien in October 1942 and which chose Laurendeau as its secretary.

Laurendeau employed many of the same arguments that had contributed to Henri Bourassa's prominence as the principal defender of French Canada's interests in the first conscription crisis of 1917. Laurendeau, however, was more inclined than Bourassa to support Quebec's nationalist and autonomist aspirations as demonstrated by his active participation in the Bloc populaire canadien. Laurendeau's keen support for increased provincial autonomy and his opposition to conscription facilitated his entry into the Bloc populaire and his eventual leadership of the Quebec provincial wing of the same party.

The emergence of the Bloc populaire contributed to popularising progressive ideas in Quebec. According to Michael Oliver, "the Bloc tended towards the left in its social proposals, for Duplessis and the Union nationale were well entrenched as the right-wing opposition to the provincial Liberal régime. ... the Bloc had to adopt both a more extreme attitude to the war and a more radical social policy" (Oliver 1991a, 197). The Bloc populaire denounced the conditions of poverty, low wages, and exploitation by trusts that afflicted Quebec while simultaneously calling for the strengthening of family life and the pursuit of increased provincial autonomy.[4]

In July 1947 Laurendeau quit the Bloc populaire in protest against the decision made by many party members to back the Union nationale. He became editor-in-chief of *Le Devoir* and, as such, one of the most influential voices in Quebec. While Laurendeau did not disagree with Duplessis on the need to protect provincial autonomy, he sharply opposed the premier's anti-modernist views on social policy (Filion 1947; Oliver 1991a, 202).

Throughout his life Laurendeau consistently promoted social justice for all. He was among the first Quebec intellectuals to support the establishment of a social security system (Monière 1983, 206, 212). Laurendeau's awareness of the central role of the labour movement in the quest for social justice convinced him of the necessity for nationalists to rally behind labour's cause (Monière 1983, 193). Ryerson said of him that "The nationalist Laurendeau was also a democrat and a humanist. The strength of his worldview arises from these latter, more global commitments. Whereas certain nationalisms incline toward chauvinism and racism, his was open to the world. Hence his ability to conceive of a synthesis of the social and the national" (1990, 221, our translation).

Laurendeau's contribution to political life increased once he joined *Le Devoir*, which provided a forum for neo-nationalist thinking at the time. Several colleagues at *Le Devoir*, such as Gérard Filion, Pierre Laporte, and Jean-Marc Léger, worked together with Laurendeau to imbue nationalism with a deeper meaning through modernisation. During the 1950s, they were the source of inspiration for many of the Liberal Federation and Quebec Liberal Party's policy proposals (Linteau et al. 1986, 332). Laurendeau's experience with the Bloc populaire canadien, where he had developed a conceptualisation of the country that could accommodate Quebec's liberal nationalists, enabled him to reconcile Quebecers to a vision of a modern and pluralist Quebec within Canada.

Following his return from Europe, Laurendeau popularised the French personalist ideas of Jacques Maritain and Emmanuel Mounier in Quebec. Pierre Trudeau and Marcel Rioux followed his example, illustrating the extent to which Laurendeau, Rioux, and Trudeau were not so distant from one another at the time. So much so in Trudeau's case that Michael Oliver wrote in 1956 in *The Passionate Debate*:

> But Trudeau and his associates have many affinities with at least part of Québec's nationalist tradition. The most obvious, perhaps, is the debt which, like *La Relève*, they owe to *Esprit*. ... *Cité Libre's* preoccupation with social and economic conditions is associated with a belief in socialism. As socialists, its *équipe* finds more allies among convinced nationalists than in any other segments of the French Canadian intelligentsia. (1991a, 206–7)[5]

It is in the area of social policy that Quebec's progressive forces converged, though they frequently clashed on the issue of nationalism. In one of his most important articles, published in *Le Devoir* in 1953, Laurendeau made the argument that "The nationalists must, while remaining firm in their essential positions, found their organisation on more universal ideas. The first of these, in the contemporary context and in our specific situation, is the idea of social welfare. ... It could serve as a link with groups of another ethnic origin" (Laurendeau, *Le Devoir*, 14 August, 1953 quoted in Oliver, 1991a, 221).

According to Pierre Anctil, Laurendeau's search for universal values led him to pursue an ethno-cultural *rapprochement* with non French-Canadian components of Quebec and Canada at large. In Anctil's words, Laurendeau was "the first francophone intellectual to defend in the pages of a reputed newspaper the idea of a cultural convergence between old-stock Québécois and post-war immigrants" (1990, 233, our translation). Such a goal was central to Laurendeau's perception of the emerging nation which he envisioned as open to world values.

Laurendeau's contribution was long-lasting in the area of community-building. In a noted editorial in *Le Devoir* of 20 January 1962, he recommended the establishment of a Royal Commission to settle Canada's constitutional problems. Maurice Lamontagne[6] who, at an earlier time, had convinced Marcel Rioux to assume the leadership of the Institut canadien d'affaires publiques, felt that the best available person to chair such a commission was Laurendeau himself.

Shortly thereafter, Prime Minister Lester B. Pearson saw a good opportunity and invited Laurendeau to co-chair with Davidson

Dunton the Royal Commission on Bilingualism and Biculturalism which was formally created on 23 July 1963. Considering that its main focus was on Canada's two principal languages and two founding cultures, Laurendeau could hardly have refused such an invitation.

This brief historical review reveals some important high points in Laurendeau's career and provides the necessary background information to understand the influence he had and continues to have on a number of his contemporaries. The role he played within Jeune-Canada, his time in France, his work at *L'Action nationale* and later with *Le Devoir*, his participation in La ligue pour la défense du Canada, Le Bloc populaire canadien, and the Royal Commission on Bilingualism and Biculturalism all contributed to developing the principal foundations of his political thought. Indeed, one can clearly identify two main principles: first, a blend of individual and community liberalism and, second, the pursuit of political equality and the quest for an egalitarian society founded on social justice. These two principles are examined in the remainder of this chapter.

BLENDING INDIVIDUAL AND COMMUNITY LIBERALISM

Laurendeau did not embrace the atomistic view of society according to which each individual is said to represent a self-sufficient whole, apart from any larger community to which he or she may belong. Rather, he insisted on the importance of the ties that bind each individual to his or her community. In Laurendeau's view, the community and the nation give meaning to an individual's life and provide a necessary context for individual freedom and personal fulfillment.

Laurendeau consistently defined Quebec as a nation, rejecting the premise that it is "a province like any other." He believed, however, that federalism could accommodate Canada's two dominant cultures and he felt throughout most of his public life that the future of francophones was best protected under a federal constitution that allowed for a strong Quebec state. For example, on 30 September 1949 he wrote in *Le Devoir* on the essence of federalism and the threat posed by Ottawa's centralist tendencies. For Laurendeau, Ottawa centralists calling themselves federalists was an abuse of language. Their political designs, if unchecked, would destroy confederation by undermining the balance between governing powers. Quebec had to remain vigilant to avoid falling prey to the "horse trades" proposed by Ottawa (Laurendeau 1973, 131–132).

This does not mean that Laurendeau maintained a blind loyalty to federalism and all things federal. His convictions were much more complex as illustrated by his participation in the Bloc populaire canadien and the Royal Commission on Bilingualism and Biculturalism. Paul-André Comeau comments that during the hearings and deliberations of the Bilingualism and Biculturalism Commission in the 1960s, Laurendeau expressed frustration with the apparent indifference of anglophones and admiration for René Lévesque's strong position in the dialogue with "the other Canada" (Comeau 1990, 21).

In his diary, Laurendeau also noted that "In the company of certain anglophones, I feel driven toward separatism: 'They're too stupid, they'd only give in the face of strength.' But when I come back here, the separatists drive me back into the arms of Canada: they're either too naive, too far from political reality, or curiously unstable and superficial" (Laurendeau [February 22, 1964] 1990, 75, our translation). He also wrote: "At present I confess that when left to myself I experience separatist urges several times a week and even several times a day. These seem to be elemental emotional reactions to which I do not attribute more importance than is necessary" (Laurendeau [May 2, 1964] 1990, 174, our translation). Despite his flirtations with separatism, Laurendeau stopped short of overt displays of support. He remained simultaneously a committed Québécois and Canadian. His dual identity is consistently reflected throughout his writings. Laurendeau never gave up on national reconciliation, always searching for a way out of the Canadian political quagmire.

In Book 1 of the General Introduction to the *Report of the Royal Commission on Bilingualism and Biculturalism*, known as the *Blue Pages*, which Laurendeau allegedly wrote, he uses the example of the artist's relationship to society to make the point that every individual is a product of his or her society, without being reduced to this. Art is an exercise in futility if the artist is not able to speak meaningfully to the broader community. And to do that, the artist must be integrated into that community (Canada 1967, xxvi).

Laurendeau also wrote in the *Blue Pages* that "Social relations in the world today are very complex and take in much more than the sum of personal behaviour. To understand them we must, in a sense, 'depersonalise' them, and bring to light the mechanisms by which social groups (ethnic, cultural, or others) live side by side, integrate or separate, according to the different types of activities which men carry on" (Canada 1967, xl). The complementary nature of the individual and the community was made clear throughout Laurendeau's account of one of Canada's worst constitutional crises.

Laurendeau's understanding of the relationship between individual and community led him to develop a liberal version of nationalism. According to Monière, Laurendeau's theory of nationalism is based on a hierarchy of concepts that brings together God, family, the nation, and the state. Summarising Laurendeau's philosophy, Monière wrote:

> God is the first principle who creates man and places him in a natural environment. Then the family does its part by making everyone into a person and giving everyone an identity. But the family by itself is not sufficient for ensuring personality development. It has to do its work within a larger context: the nation. The nation is defined as a collectivity of men capable of communicating among each other because of the sharing not only of a common culture but also of ways of thinking, feeling and acting. In the final analysis, the state is the nation organized ... He declares it a matter of principle that the individual cannot exist without the nation, for it is this latter that bequeaths culture to him ... For Laurendeau, culture is at the core of the nation. (Monière 1983, 70, our translation)

This particular understanding of the nation supported liberal values and assisted in transforming the dominant nationalist view from one that was inward-looking to one that was sensitive to universal changes and willing to challenge established value systems. This transformation led to the emergence of what has been termed a "neo-nationalist" tendency that became the principal source of inspiration of the Quiet Revolution.[7] Acknowledging that two concurrent ideologies, namely neo-nationalism and *Cité libre* liberalism, fought for the hearts and minds of Québécois following World War II, Behiels writes: "Slow to be recognized but in many ways the first to take root in Québec was the ideology of neo-nationalism. This significant metamorphosis of French-Canadian nationalism had its origins in the Bloc Populaire Canadien movement" (1985, 5–6). We have noted already the key role played by Laurendeau in the creation of the Bloc populaire canadien.

It is crucial to stress that Laurendeau believed that the community of reference for French Canadians was necessarily Quebec. He wrote, "Quebec is the capital of French Canada. In a certain sense, and indeed without a doubt, the Québec state is the national state of French Canadians" (Laurendeau [November 1961] 1970, 40, our translation). However, Laurendeau was aware of potential repercussions of nationalism on the life of French Canadians. He argued, when assessing whether Quebec needed its own delegations overseas, that

> The more the Quebec state becomes "national," at least in terms of its intentions (and the functions of a national state transcend the cultural order), and the more its weakness and limitations become apparent, the more power and money it will demand to meet its increasingly better defined goals. Thus policies that began in order to help francophone minorities in other provinces may lead us, over the long haul, towards secession. (Laurendeau [November 1961] 1970, 42, our translation)

While Laurendeau believed that an ideal solution for French Canadians would be based on the convergence of individual and collective values within the federal framework of Canada, secession remained a possibility. His belief that Canada could be built on cooperating rather than competing values was an important innovation.

THE PURSUIT OF POLITICAL EQUALITY AND SOCIAL JUSTICE

The second tenet of Laurendeau's political thought is the pursuit of equality and, through it, the achievement of social justice. His nationalism was motivated by a deep commitment to the redress of social and political inequities. Monière is of the opinion that "André Laurendeau's nationalism embodied a visceral rejection of discrimination and a passionate desire for equality" (1983, 192, our translation).

Laurendeau's notion of equality first takes into account the individual-collective dimension that we discussed above. In the General Introduction of Book 1 of the Royal Commission on Bilingualism and Biculturalism report, one reads: "Individual equality can fully exist only if each community has, throughout the country, the means to progress within its culture and to express that culture. To this end it will have its own institutions in certain fields, while in other sectors it will be free to participate, on satisfactory terms, in common institutions and agencies" (xliv). In other words, individual equality is attainable only through the equality of communities. According to Stanley Bréhaut Ryerson, for Laurendeau equality "no longer concerns cultural development and the development of individuals, but rather the degree of self-determination available to a given society in relation to another" (1990, 220, our translation).

Although for Laurendeau there are many distinct types of equality that need to be pursued if the dignity and freedom of a community's members are to be protected, the one that recurs throughout the majority of his writings involves equality between Canada's "two founding peoples." Going back to 1932 when Laurendeau recited the Manifesto of the 'Young Generation' before an important gathering of 2,000 people, which turned out to be the founding meeting of the Jeune-Canada movement, the equality-of-peoples principle was already well-established in his mind. He was also aware of the need to foster mutual respect between French and English, and to put forward reasonable demands for change in this direction. "We have no intention of resurrecting old hatreds. On the contrary, we believe that the only way to maintain the moderate nature of legitimate French-Canadian nationalism is to ensure a scrupulous respect within each of the two races for the other." For Laurendeau this was the political insight and heritage bequeathed by the Fathers of Confederation, and it should be the guidepost for renegotiating the place of French Canadians within Canadian society and within the Canadian state. "Equitable representation within all federal ministries" was an essential starting point" (Le Manifeste de la jeune génération, 17 December 1932 cited in Monière 1983, 51–2, our translation).

Laurendeau and the 'Young Generation' group were already speaking out against unfair practices within the federal state and were calling for changes. Prime Minister R.B. Bennett's government was denounced as completely insensitive toward French-Canadians' desires to have access to jobs within the federal civil service (Horton 1992, 34). Corrective measures were long in coming as French Canadians waited until the late 1960s before changes to the federal civil service were implemented. In a brief to the Special Joint Committee of the Senate and of the House of Commons on the Constitution of Canada on 30 March 1971, Léon Dion indicated the urgency with which the federal government needed to enact corrective measures at the middle-management level positions of its own workforce. Indeed, "less than 15 percent of them [100,000 jobs] are held by French-speakers at the present time. This means that 1,500 additional recruits would have to be hired each year to reach a level of 30% in ten years; yet this is the minimum number required to create a French working environment and an adequate pool of talent from which to draw French-speaking senior officials" (Dion 1973, 257).

Laurendeau was in complete agreement with Dion's conclusions. It is worth noting that Laurendeau was one of the first Quebec intellectuals to suggest changes in this direction in order to reconcile Canadian duality. Michael Behiels remarked appropriately that

> French Canadians had to be made welcome in all federal institutions and departments and those agencies had to serve francophones in their maternal language. Overly preoccupied with internal Québec developments, the Cité-libristes found little time to devote to the pursuit of liberal objectives at the federal level. Ironically, it would take a neo-nationalist, André Laurendeau, to turn Cité-libristes in that direction in the early sixties. (1985, 273–4)

In addition to being concerned by the minority position of French Canadians within their own country, Laurendeau felt, along with Marcel Rioux and George Grant,[8] that the American cultural monolith south of border represented an even greater threat. Laurendeau said that "The danger in all its amplitude comes from the presence beside us of the United States – a culture which surrounds us, leans on us, infiltrates us, and is embodied in a people who are numerous and rich. With them beside us, it is no longer one against two but one against thirty. This disproportion would remain even if Québec became independent" (Laurendeau 1973 [8 March 1961], 185). Laurendeau wrote those lines at a time when nationalist and secessionist sentiments in Quebec were ascendant and when Canada's prime minister, John Diefenbaker was governing Canada without much concern for Quebec (Laurendeau 1973 [May 1962], 197–201).

Laurendeau was equally preoccupied with the economic and cultural threat of the United States. His concerns with Americanisation and, more broadly, imperialism, remain constant throughout his public life, dating back to the 1930s. He also expressed opposition to Canada's imitation of American foreign policy. He felt that Canada was ill-advised to enter the North Atlantic Treaty Organization in 1949 (Horton 1992, 151).

Laurendeau believed that the cultural threat emanating from the United States was more immediate than the threat posed by Canadian demographics. He was of the view that Quebec was as threatened by Americanisation as was English Canada and that the alliance of the two Canadas was as critical for the survival of Quebec as it was for English Canada. This led many Quebec separatists, including Pierre Bourgault, to challenge Laurendeau and to accuse him of having "lost the faith" and not understanding the "logic" of independence (Laurendeau 1973 [8 March 1961], 184). Laurendeau believed that biculturalism could solidify Canada's cultural position in North America. But Laurendeau also felt that Canada's problems would diminish the day Québécois have a Canadian counterpart, another people with whom they can enter into a dialogue. In an article entitled "The Anglo-Canadian Nation?" he wrote perceptively: "It is possible to imagine that to protect itself against the troubles in Québec, English Canada might forge a new sense of unity and learn to define itself once again. Then we would have someone to talk to and they could talk back, and the battle would be fierce. But that would be better, it seems to me, than messing around in the kind of swamp we are all bogged down in now" (Laurendeau 1973 [July 1963], 243).

In the 1967 General Introduction of the *Report on Bilingualism and Biculturalism*, Laurendeau summarised the Commissioners' bicultural and binational view of Canada.

We have already said the two dominant cultures in Canada are embodied in distinct societies, and that the word 'society' designates 'the types of organization and the institutions that a rather large population, inspired by a common culture, has created for itself or has received, and which it freely manages over quite a vast territory, where it lives as a homogeneous group according to common standards and rules of conduct.' We recognized the main elements of a distinct French-speaking society in Québec. The same may be said of the other culture in the English-speaking provinces. (Canada 1967, xxxiii)

In other words, both the French- and English-speaking societies of Canada were seen by Laurendeau and his fellow commissioners to be distinct. Moreover, the minority status of the English-speaking community within Quebec was significantly ameliorated both by their membership in the broader English-speaking society beyond Quebec's borders, and by "a very advantageous socio-economic position" (xxxiii).

The dominant economic position occupied by Quebec anglophones, to which Laurendeau refers in the above passage, acted as a catalyst for Québécois' demands for more favourable terms within Canada's federal system. The quest for socio-economic equality became a central objective of the Quiet Revolution and encouraged many nationalists in favour of independent status for Quebec.

Laurendeau argued that "The life of the two cultures implies in principle the life of the two languages. Later, when we deal with the idea of equality, we shall see that, at the practical level, an attempt to make possible provision for cultural equality is primarily an attempt to make every possible provision for linguistic equality" (Canada, Book 1, 1967, xxxviii). This pursuit of equality indicates a favourable bias toward minority groups in Canada at large as well as within its regions (Book 1, 1967, xlvi) and paves the way to social justice.

The quest for social justice completes the second tenet of Laurendeau's political thought. Even before his return from France in 1937, one can see that Laurendeau had established the foundations of his thought. In the context of the Spanish Civil War, he contributed an important article to the January issue of *L'Action nationale* in which he stated: "We do not confuse in vain, for decades, eternal life with an outdated social system. God is not the bourgeois police charged to defend the land of nobles and religious communities, nor capitalism's brazen exploitation of the poor" (Laurendeau cited in Monière 1983, 96, our translation).

Laurendeau's political philosophy could be defined as that of a "liberal reformist," to use Linteau et al.'s description (1986, 332). In his vision of a modern Quebec society, Laurendeau rejected the lineage of blood and spoke of the necessity to develop on the basis of high democratic principles.

In his demands for social justice Laurendeau repeatedly denounced exploitative practices and sided with the weakest (Oliver 1991a, 210). However, it never occurred to him to compare the socio-economic conditions of Québécois to those experienced by African communities, as frequently was done by, for example, contributors to more radical journals such as *Parti Pris*. While the decolonization debate was raging in Quebec, Laurendeau kept his distance and wrote: "These men felt despised like we have never been. They know poverty like we have never known" (Laurendeau cited in Bourgault 1982, 23, our translation).

Denouncing prejudices, Laurendeau wrote, "I detest the fact that it is necessary to mobilise ten thousand troops to allow a Black student to take courses at Oxford University, in the old state of Mississippi. I find it appalling that men who now attack the dignity of man possess the rancorous conviction that they have had their rights infringed when their government snatches their prey away from them" (Laurendeau [December 1962] 1970, 105, our translation). Michael Oliver said aptly that "Laurendeau's sympathies were with those who sought freedom from economic exploitation in Spain and Ethiopia as well as Québec ... He was egalitarian in his criticisms of an economic system which erected privileges of wealth; he was libertarian in his unwillingness to sacrifice personal fulfilment for the sake of collective order" (1991a, 210).

CONCLUSION

André Laurendeau's contributions to political discourse in Quebec and Canada have left a lasting legacy – capturing both the particular realities of his time as well as enduring questions concerning the Quebec/Canada impasse today. His post-World War II thought in particular served to inspire the Quiet Revolution and later provided an important political framework upon which scholars tackling Quebec's existential question in Canada continue to draw. Perhaps Laurendeau's most significant contribution lies in his conception of equality as flowing from the recognition of Quebec as a founding nation in Canada. For Laurendeau, individuals could only be conceived of as truly free and equal across Canada if their respective national communities are permitted to coexist and deliberate as equal partners. Moreover, Laurendeau consistently emphasized an open and outward-looking expression of Quebec nationalism, open to social change, during an era in which many of his contemporaries viewed nationalist movements as backward and inherently conservative. It was through this unique blend of nationalism and liberalism that Laurendeau was able to put forth the idea that Canada be built upon cooperating rather than competing values between the two majority groups. For Laurendeau, social justice went hand in hand with nationalism to the extent that the Quebec state, as the engine of a modern and secular national movement, was the only viable and effective agent of progressive change for Québécois.

Laurendeau's impact was also pronounced in defining the boundaries of the Quebec nation. He sought to redefine the criteria for belonging to Quebec society along universal values and promoted cultural convergence between Québécois and post-war immigrants. Perhaps the most significant pillar of such universal values was social welfare, which Laurendeau believed could serve as a link between a variety of cultures and identities in Quebec. Indeed, for Laurendeau, nationalism and social justice need not be opposite aims – as some cosmopolitan thinkers suggested. Rather, they complemented each other to the extent that constructing a national community as an intellectual and practical exercise allowed Laurendeau to envision social justice as an integral aspect of the project. For Laurendeau, nation-building, or the affirmation of Quebec as constituting a distinct cultural space in an equal partnership with the rest of Canada, was not an end in itself. As the co-chair of the Royal Commission on Bilingualism and Biculturalism, Laurendeau sought to cement this duality by promoting the inclusion of French Canadians in federal institutions and framing a federal constitution that allowed for a strong Quebec state. A country built along Canada's two dominant cultures would serve not only to provide the necessary context for individual freedom and ambitious community/social initiatives across Canada, but would also act as a strong bulwark to the omnipresent threat of American cultural encroachment, which was another of Laurendeau's concerns. Nationalist, communitarian, and liberal, Laurendeau's contributions to both the substance of Quebec nationalism as well as Quebec's place in Canada remain with us to this day.

CHAPTER FIVE

Personal Emancipation, Pluralism, and Community: The Egalitarian Vision of Marcel Rioux

We can imagine democracy as a system of government, but we can also examine it from a broader perspective as a collection of ideas relating to mankind and its destiny. Moreover, the central premise of democracy is that no decision is ever permanent, that mankind can change the course of events, that he has the means to affect history. As Jeanne Hersch wrote in *Idéologie et réalité* "the fundamental value of democracy is the human person, irreducible and insurmountable – it being understood that this is not like a centre of possibilities or liberty – in other words it is, at a philosophical level, an internal and unpredictable necessity, and at a political level, preserved indecision." (Rioux 1960, 3–4, 13, our translation)

THE COMMUNITY LIBERALISM OF MARCEL RIOUX

The name Marcel Rioux is not as well-known to Canadians as those of Pierre Trudeau or Charles Taylor, but it is firmly associated with Quebec's quest for autonomy and self-assertion in the North American space. Marcel Rioux's influence on Quebec society cannot be conceived independently of the political and intellectual contexts with which he often found himself at odds.

Over the course of his lifetime Rioux espoused many causes, but always situated himself on the side of the exploited, the dominated, and the marginal. Although his contributions to Quebec intellectual thought are many, we intend to focus on Rioux's understanding of the concepts of liberty, equality, and community as they constitute the basis of his understanding of the Good Life and the Good Society.

Born in Amqui, a small town of the Matapedia valley, in 1919, Rioux has always supported the way of life characteristic of small communities. Reminiscing on the time he spent there, Rioux noted the absence of class consciousness (Duchastel, 1981: 13) and the presence of a rich community life. As an anthropologist, Rioux felt that small communities formed the basis of social and political life in a given country, and that power ought to emerge from below rather than being imposed from above.

Rioux went on to complete his classical college education in Rimouski in the early 1930s, where he broke with religion. In sharp opposition to the conservative values circulating at the time, Rioux chose to quench his thirst for critical knowledge by reading Social Credit documents as well as *Action libérale nationale's* literature (Duchastel 1981, 16). At the same time that he discovered the French journal, *Esprit*, a monthly publication founded by the personalist Emmanuel Mounier in 1932, which argued in favour of socially progressive Catholicism. As noted earlier, Quebec's intellectuals were influenced by Mounier and Jacques Maritain at the time. Cases in point include Pierre Trudeau and André Laurendeau. However, in contrast to Trudeau, who accepted the critique of the nation-state and nationalism expounded by the personalists, Rioux was much more prone to take into account the importance of community life and the preconditions for social solidarity. He refused to condemn systematically nationalist projects, as he believed that there may be a just cause behind such political movements.

Rioux quickly came to identify with the Left. The first manifestation of his left leanings took place during the Spanish Civil War when he sided with the Republicans in their struggle against fascism (Rioux 1990a, 27–8). His desire to discover "the" truth led him, after graduation from classical college, to become a journalist. It is highly probable that the high esteem in which he held Olivar Asselin contributed to his first career choice. He excluded the choices of lawyer, medical doctor, or priest because he considered such establishment professions to be on the side of the exploiters (Duchastel 1981, 17–18).

In 1939, Rioux's academic path led him to study for a period of one year in Ottawa under the Dominicans, during which time he renewed his friendship with Maurice Lamontagne and Maurice Tremblay. His friends introduced him to Marius Barbeau, a renowned ethnologist/anthropologist in the employ of the National Museum of Canada, and soon to become his father-in-law. A year later, Rioux moved to Montreal, where he registered at the École des Hautes Études Commerciales (HEC) and took some evening courses in philosophy. He quickly gave up his commercial degree to complete his studies in philosophy, obtaining a degree in 1941. After this one year interval in Montreal, he returned to Ottawa where he obtained a job in the civil service. It is at that time that his identification with Quebec started to take shape. Opposing right-wing nationalists, Rioux had already come to the conclusion that nationalism could be beneficial and could contribute to the advancement of progressive ideas. More a libertarian than a left nationalist, Rioux felt that nothing was preordained and that the world of social possibilities (*possibles*) was limitless. This optimistic view would animate him throughout most of his life.

Immediately after the Second World War, Rioux was part of the first group of Quebec students to take up residency in France. At that time he had frequent contact with Pierre Trudeau. The two shared a visceral dislike for clerical Quebec and a deep opposition to the prevailing ideology of conservatism. They intended to return to Quebec to fight Duplessis and his regime (Duchastel 1981, 43–6). Many years later, Rioux would publicly condemn Trudeau for his political actions.[1] They were companions-in-struggle as long as their common enemy was Duplessis and the old regime. But with the end of that regime, they would gravitate toward quite different political camps.

Rioux left Paris to come back to Ottawa in 1948 to work as an anthropologist for the Ottawa museum. The Catholic Church, which controlled entry to teaching positions in Quebec universities, was not inclined to favour Rioux whose left-wing ideas and atheist views disqualified him as a candidate (Duchastel 1981, 86). Indeed, Rioux was denied a position at Laval University and at the University of Montreal because of his agnosticism (Dion 1993, 131, note 17, 176–7).

It is at that time that he began paying more attention to the place occupied by small communities in the political and social processes.

He studied eleven anthropological fields between 1948 and 1958. His early work is already indicative of his life-long inclination to studying small communities. His fieldwork led him to conceive Quebec's culture as the sum of small units and distinct cultural processes. He favoured a microscopic approach to explaining social and political phenomena, suspicious as he was of global interpretations. Among the small communities studied, one notes his works on Aboriginal peoples in the 1950's (Rioux 1951b, 1955b) revealing his early interest in cultural diversity. However, like most of his contemporaries, Rioux's principal research focus was not to be the First Nations.

Until 1956 Rioux generally kept clear of public life, limiting his interventions to radio and television interviews. That year was a watershed for Rioux. It was then that he became an intellectual *engagé*. He became an active member of the Co-operative Commonwealth Federation (CCF) and assumed the direction of the Institut canadien d'affaires publiques (ICAP). He had been introduced to the group by Maurice Lamontagne and Pierre Trudeau, who at that stage of this life was a socialist activist (Rioux 1990a, 68). Rioux's agnostic and left leanings were rapidly crystallizing into a political philosophy (Duchastel, 1981: 79). He started questioning the value of scientific knowledge and of field specialization. He was interested in the notion of colonization, which would become, in his thinking, the key explanatory variable accounting for Quebec's lagging development.

Through his continued contacts with Trudeau, who was then working for the Privy Council in Ottawa, Rioux was encouraged to contribute articles from time to time to *Cité libre* (1951a, 1953, 1955a, 1960, 1961). While Rioux did not adhere to the federalist leaning of the journal, he shared its objectives of social criticism. Rioux's first two contributions dealt with secondary education, while the third one, for which he received the Parizeau medal awarded by the Association canadienne-française pour l'avancement des sciences, concerned the development of ideologies and crisis of conscience in French Canada. His last two contributions to *Cité libre* were a response to Trudeau's depiction of French Canadians as steeped in an anti-democratic tradition (Rioux 1960), and a political statement in which Rioux toyed with new options for Quebec, including the need to create a provincial third party on the left that would be committed to independence in order to transform Quebec into a more equitable society (Rioux 1961).

It was Rioux's obsession with overturning Duplessis' anti-liberal and regressive vision that had led him to continue his affiliation with Trudeau. However, he began to distance himself from Trudeau in the early 1960's when it became clear that Trudeau was willing to sacrifice his socialist commitments in exchange for public office. Rioux himself was never a political opportunist, preferring to pursue his social and political agenda from outside the power structure. Nor was Rioux a politician at heart. Pierre Trudeau, in his dedication to Rioux in "The Asbestos Strike," wrote: "À mon ami Marcel Rioux, anthropophage distingué, et camarade sans pareil, dans l'espoir que cette lecture le métamorphose enfin en ZOONPOLITIA (N.D.R. en homme politique). Pierre E.T., juin 1956" (Duchastel 1981, 82–3).

Following the defeat of the Union Nationale in June 1960, Rioux no longer saw *Cité libre* as a vehicle of social criticism but rather as a journal serving the interests of a new elite (Rioux 1960, 1961). His restless search for liberty, equality, and fraternity led him to break away from the journal and to resign as director of the Institut canadien des affaires publiques (ICAP) shortly after the 1960 election of Lesage's Liberals. He believed that an independent Quebec, founded on a socialist platform, was the most promising alternative for the future. Moreover, his desire to continue fighting clericalism, and his denunciation of the continued exploitation of the toiling masses, along with the treatment of francophones as an "ethnic class," were not shared by many members of the ICAP group. This led to Rioux's withdrawal from the organization, most of the members of which rallied around either the federal or the provincial Liberal party (Rioux 1990a, 69).

A reformist, secularist, and socialist, Rioux felt that the ideology of *rattrapage* (catching-up) that had taken hold of Quebec in the 1960s was simply a quest for individualism, and that the fight for egalitarianism had lost its political relevance. He felt that this was one of the manifestations, affecting both Quebec and Canada, of creeping Americanization. Rather than hoping that Quebec would "catch-up" with the model of economic development in the rest of Canada and the United States, Rioux hoped that Quebec would forge its own model as a just society in which social and political equality were the redundant fundamental principles. The idea of "surpassing one's self" or *dépassement*[2] became his leitmotif.

Rioux formally broke with *rattrapage* supporters in 1961. Instead, he developed a three-pronged ideological model of society: traditional, transitional (*rattrapage*), and participatory (later termed *dépassement*). Rioux examined the extent to which the writings of Karl Marx applied to the Quebec situation. Never totally at ease with Marxist interpretations, he nonetheless adopted the marxian concepts of "contradiction" and "superstructure" as relevant for understanding the Quebec situation. As a man on a quest for the national liberation for his people, Rioux sought to reconcile Marxism and nationalism, while declining to join the "Althusserian" camp of Marxist intellectuals who rapidly came to dominate the social sciences in Quebec. Instead, Rioux developed his own critical cultural sociology, based on the notion of alienation so central in Marxist thought.

Rioux's contributions to a redefinition of Quebec/Canada relations, as well as to Quebec's place in the continental economy, was adhered to by a rapidly growing number of intellectuals, especially among the most progressive forces. In the 1960s, the pursuit of national liberation was a highly moral and legitimate objective, especially in light of the many African colonies that were freeing themselves from their colonizers. Such a quest was emulated by many Quebec intellectuals. In 1964 Rioux, too, openly declared his support for Quebec independence. However, he rejected the idea of armed struggle, as promoted by the Front de libération du Québec (FLQ). Instead he believed that the democratic process was the best means by which the independence movement could achieve its goals.

Rioux, as we mentioned earlier, was already active within the left. Having backed the CCF, he was a natural supporter of the creation of New Democratic Party in 1961. It is in this context that he came in contact with progressive Quebec anglophones such as Michael Oliver, Charles Taylor, and Jack Weldon, all professors at McGill University. Rioux was of the opinion that the NDP should concentrate its energies at the federal level. This led him and others to create in 1962 the Parti socialiste du Québec (PSQ), a party based on the fusion of nationalist and socialist agendas. Building on two streams of left tendencies (intellectual and unionist), he joined forces with Jacques Dofny (University of Montreal), Émile Boudreau

(Fédération des travailleurs du Québec) and Rolland Martel (Confédération des syndicats nationaux) to found *Socialisme 64* (Rioux 1990a, 110–11). Rioux did not join another rising political movement, the *Rassemblement pour l'indépendance nationale* (RIN), since he was suspicious of its right-wing component (which included André d'Allemagne and Marcel Chaput). He did agree to serve, however, in RIN leader Pierre Bourgault's shadow cabinet which also included Fernand Dumont and Michel Van Schendel (Duchastel 1981, 107).

As previously noted, Rioux's interest in the field of education was significant, and he was appointed president of the Commission of Inquiry on Arts *(Commission sur l'enseignement des arts au Québec)* on which he served from 1966 until the tabling of its final report in 1968. The work accomplished by the commission assisted him greatly in developing his view on the emancipatory potential of artistic creation. This interest in the arts would become a central theme permeating his work during the 1970s and 1980s.[3]

In 1968, in the wake of further political developments, Rioux gave his support to the newly founded Parti Québécois. He perceived the growth of a counter-culture as well as the emergence of what could become the party of national independence. Conscious that he could be accused of "selling out" and betraying his socialist convictions, he responded by stating that he was giving priority to the "common front" struggle to found a new country with all of its potentialities. He also believed that the PQ's social democratic programme was acceptable to many Quebecers.

At the time that Rioux endorsed the Parti Québécois in 1968, he had already acquired and developed the three philosophical principles that would guide his subsequent thinking: liberty, equality, and community. Equivalent to the three great ideals of the French Revolution (liberty, equality, fraternity), these concepts were applied rigorously by Rioux and were the backbone to his understanding of the many crises that were yet to be experienced by advanced liberal democracies, including Canada and Quebec (Rioux 1990a, 62–3).

CULTURE

Rioux's interpretation of Quebec's dependence was associated with the domination of Quebec, economically and socially, by English Canadians and Americans (Rioux [1969, 1977] 1987, 1974, 150–6).

He was particularly concerned by the continental hegemonic position of capitalism which he considered a major impediment to Quebec's self-expression (Rioux 1974, 170). However, Rioux remained confident that Quebec's youth was on the side of the cultural revolution[4] and that they, like no other group, could "surpass themselves" and develop new codes of conduct and value structures. There is an indication here that for Rioux real change begins not in the political sphere but in the everyday activities of the common citizen (1974, 175–7).

Rioux was also particularly concerned with the issue of social inequality in Canada. In collaboration with Jacques Dofny he developed the "ethnic class" thesis that established the extent to which social classes in Canada are structured ethnically with English Canadians occupying the higher positions and French Canadians allocated more menial tasks (Rioux and Dofny 1962; Rioux 1965).

This leads us to look at Rioux's complex understanding of culture, since it is around culture, that he articulated the concepts of liberty, equality, and community. Culture became particularly important for Rioux by the end of the 1960s, after which time he had turned decisively toward a type of critical sociology that privileged culture as the object of analysis. Culture constitutes a guiding thread throughout Rioux's work. He constantly fine-tuned his interpretation of culture throughout his career, to the point of devising five complementary meanings of the word, three of which are central to the present account: culture-heritage, culture-structure, and culture-transcendance or *culture-dépassement*.[5]

Rioux argued that all communities are experiencing these three cultural expressions at different rhythms and in distinct fashions. Culture-heritage refers to the national histories that peoples transmit from generation to generation. Culture-structure refers to learned codes and illustrates the extent to which culture constitutes a buffer against social chaos. Culture-transcendance is the most important level of the three for Rioux, as it recognizes the central role of individuals as agents of change in everyday life, as well as in their political actions.

Concurring with Piaget, Rioux maintained in the Report of the Tribunal on Culture, that

> Man, because he possesses the faculty of self-transformation, is determined neither from the outside nor from the inside to act in such-and-such a manner; he can create his own structure of behaviour ... we must ponder

the cultural possibilities rather than the preservation of heritage or culture-code ... If, in other historical periods, cultural development meant the transcendance of historical conditions, innovation, creation and consciouness-raising, how much more so is this true and necessary for us today! (Rioux, Loiselle, Loranger, Jutra, Bouchard and Godin 1975, 46–7)

Rioux referred to culture-transcendance to support his claim that Quebec regions, communities, and Quebecers in general have to pursue sovereignty to free themselves from dependence and imagine their own cultural and political space. This new cultural formation would lead to a truly self-governed society. Contrary to other authors in the critical tradition, for whom all rootedness in time and space is contrary to liberty and must be overcome, Rioux criticized the onesidedness of both the modernizers, who celebrated only the present, and conservatives, who did the same with the past (Rioux 1990a, 101). Rioux accorded special attention to socio-historical particularity because of his own epistomelogical bias towards practice rather than theory.

Rioux's critical sociology brings together liberty, equality, and community in a unique way. It is premised on the assertion that human history is an act of imagination and self-creation; that humans are capable of changing their own lives, as well as their society, in the face of all the inherited limits and determinisms that bind and frustrate them. This was a revolutionary philosophy of human agency. Above all, it is Rioux's notion of culture-transcendance that is key to his thought, since it is this that brings the troika of liberty, equality, and community life within the grasp of all human societies (Rioux 1978a, 14–15).

LIBERTY

According to Rioux, liberty is manifested in emancipatory practices (education, artistic creation, popular culture, protest movements, etc.) and manifests itself in autonomy (self-emancipation, self-creation, self-management, and reappropriation are the terms most often used). However, far from being considered in a purely individualistic or anarchistic sense, this autonomy is situated in a social context. It is an egalitarian freedom that is unimaginable without a plurality of differentiated communities.

Rioux believed that freedom developed gradually through the overcoming of alienation and social determinisms (1969b, 55).

Such a view was part of Rioux's understanding at a very early phase. He felt, like the critical sociologist Georges Gurvitch, that sociology is the science of freedom (1969b, 55). Rioux found his inspiration in the critical sociology of Karl Marx. His most significant contribution pointing in this direction can be found in "Remarques sur la sociologie critique et la sociologie aseptique" (1969b), which confirms his simultaneous quest for the Good Life and the Good Society. However, once he had established the precepts of his own critical sociology, he was ready to cast a critical eye on Marxism. Rioux never accepted the structuralist and determinist variety of Marxism that swept Quebec universities from the late sixties until the early eighties.[6] Two studies of the early 1970s in particular contain the essentials of Rioux's critique of this brand of Marxism.

First, the study completed with his colleagues Lamarche and Sévigny on alienation and ideology in the daily life of Montrealers stressed the link between the micro-social and the macro-social (Rioux, Lamarche, Sévigny 1973). For Rioux, the roots of alienation are not based on interpersonal relations but rather on structural dimensions of given polities. However, he was keen to demonstrate the extent to which human beings are free to make their own choices between a variety of possibilities (*possibles*). It is the free expression of this liberty in a society that determines if (national) liberation is achievable (see Duchastel 1981, 140–3 for a longer discussion).

Second, in the *Essai de sociologie critique*, essentially completed in 1974 but published in 1978, Rioux stresses his belief in the centrality of human agency throughout history: "men make their own history and create their own society" (1978a, 175, our translation). This renders both scientific prediction based on social theory and prophecy based on "party line" a risky and misguided enterprise.

Essentially, Rioux's critical sociology has three fundamental consequences: that positive scientific interpretations cannot account for the entire socio-historical dimension of human existence (1978a, 10); that with respect to theory, praxis is sovereign, distinguishing Rioux from the Frankfurt school (1978a, 21–61); and finally, that a critical sociology that wishes to re-establish the dominance of praxis over theory ought to pay equal attention to the need to create an alternate type of society as it does to the need to critique the existing one (1978a, 5).

Between 1974 and 1978, Rioux found ways to express his world-view through his participation in the decision to create a journal of social criticism, *Possibles*,[7] in June 1974 and through his chairing of Quebec's Tribunal on Culture in 1975. The latter needs to be situated historically, as it was a response to Liberal Premier Robert Bourassa's stated objective of "cultural sovereignty" for Quebec. In reaction to this vague party slogan, a research group on cultural sovereignty was established in April 1975 and held hearings[8] in Montreal under the presidency of Rioux. The group's report argues: "cultural development refers to the conquest of human possibilities; that is to say the conquest of ever more freedom" (Rioux, Loiselle, Loranger, Jutra, Bellefleur, Bouchard, and Godin 1975, 47). The authors understood their society's challenge and task as exploring the various ways of building another type of society and culture, one that would expand and enhance human freedom. They also argued that Quebec's dependent position within Canada and lack of full sovereignty stifled artistic creation and cultural development, which tends to be perceived as a threat both to established elites and to the particular social order that is rooted in the status quo (Rioux et al. 1975, 49–50).

One can see some similarities of view with the 1969 *Report of Commission of Inquiry on the Arts* (*l'enseignement des arts*), over which Marcel Rioux also presided, and which states that "art, by definition, is liberty. It is an openness to the imagination of revivified symbols! ... The work of the arts disturbs society and challenges it, forces it to call itself into question, to situate itself in relation to new sets of values" (Commission of Inquiry on the Arts 1969, 83).

In many ways, the Tribunal on Culture stands in direct relation to the *Refus Global* of Borduas. The Tribunal argued that the very idea of cultural sovereignty was an absurdity. The commissionners asked: how could sovereignty be divided? For them, culture could not be limited to cultural matters; it has to be active at the political and economic levels in order to encourage cultural expression. Rioux's analysis of culture is a central tenet of the Report and constitutes a key pillar in the creation of *Possibles*.

Possibles released its first issue in October 1976. The journal was and still is committed to *autogestion* (self-governance) and national independence (Rioux [1969a, 1977] 1987) while keeping a critical distance from the Parti Québécois. Sovereignty was viewed as a means to achieving self-governance and to giving birth to a new society based on social democratic principles. At times, in the writings of Rioux, self-governance and self-determination become interchangeable (Rioux 1980a, 1980b). Rioux argued that "Quebec will become the type of society that we desire only if our imagination expands to the point where new desires and new possibilities emerge and point the way toward the reappropriation of ourselves, our society and our country ... a self-governing society is a perpetual platform for experimentation and creativity" (Rioux 1980b, 21, our translation).

Rioux's definition of the Good Life and the Good Society is linked to creative change and to continued deliberation (Rioux 1980b, 22; Rioux and Crean 1980, 116–17). The referendum of May 1980 provided Rioux with the opportunity to conceptualize further the relationship. With Susan Crean, he co-authored *Deux pays pour vivre: un plaidoyer*[9] in which they assert that questioning received truths and transcending contradictions are part of the apprenticeship in freedom. Starting from one's community of origins and extending outwards to larger societies and systems, one comes inexorably to question imperial domination (1980, 10).

Rioux and Crean conceived of nationalist movements as a double process of collective and individual quests for independence. One also sees here the expression of liberal nationalism that characterizes the work of Rioux. In *Deux pays pour vivre: un plaidoyer*, this point comes through at the very outset:

> it seems to us that liberation movements that cannot imagine individual emancipation as a necessary part of national liberation are incomplete, suffering from a blind spot in their conceptualization of liberation. Not only individual and national liberation, but also that of social groups are part of a broader historical movement: that of the conquest of autonomy. (Rioux and Crean 1980, 10, our translation)

Liberty cannot be achieved without the reappropriation by citizens of their society, and this is to be accomplished through concurrent processes of social emancipation. Having experienced the referendum defeat of 1980 and witnessed the *Beau risque* proposed by René Lévesque in 1984, Rioux was careful not to reduce social emancipation to political independence. The former is a much broader objective, the attainment of which requires both a strategy of critiquing those societies that countenance domination (of countries, classes, or other collectivities) and working to expand emancipatory practices that can transcend this reality and realize new possibilities "beyond that which is realizable today" (Rioux 1985, 7–8, our translation).

The work of Rioux repeatedly stresses the place of culture in the making of nations. It is with this in mind that he hoped Québécois would one day say YES to their own national project. "A culture ceases to exist when those who are carriers are submerged by other collectivities, carriers of other mental and affective structures. It dies when those who are submerged can no longer reinterpret the borrowed messages according to their own codes and create original solutions to the problems of their collective life" (Rioux and Crean 1980, 58, our translation).

Rioux was distressed by the results of 20 May 1980, but kept high hopes for the future in *Le besoin et le désir* (1984). He was particularly disappointed because of his belief that for a people to truly exist, they need to be in a position to choose their own destiny (Rioux 1982, 163). Rioux was disappointed by inroads made by capitalist ideology and consumerism in North America and elsewhere, and was devastated by the signing of the Free Trade agreement with the United States and later with its extension to Mexico. In these developments, he saw signs that the objective of social emancipation was receding, perhaps even facing an insurmountable challenge. Nevertheless, he believed that social and political emancipation through local, regional, and national initiatives was, though modest in potential impact, the only means available to limit the damage (Rioux 1990a, 316).

EQUALITY

The quest for equality is the second key element of Rioux's personal philosophy and is constantly present in his work. As we indicated in the preceding section, Rioux insisted upon a close linkage between liberty and equality. Although the two are intertwined, there are unfortunately many cases in history where they have not cohabited comfortably. A case in point is provided by nineteenth-century England, which simultaneously stressed some individual freedoms while supporting aristocratic practices (Rioux 1964, 88).

This search for both liberty and equality led Rioux to support socialism. He argued, as early as 1964, that "the basic project of socialism has been and remains the extension of democracy – liberty and equality – into the economic and social regime. It aims at eliminating the antinomy between political democracy and the capitalist economy" (Rioux 1964, 88). This is a dominant theme that suffuses his writings.

The pursuit of equality and justice that Rioux applied at the individual level has as its precondition the equality between national communities. Unchecked liberalism can destroy communitarianism. From this emerges his critique of American imperialism and his continued insistence on a redefinition of the relationship between Quebec and the rest of Canada to confront this threat. In conjunction with Susan Crean, Rioux asked, "What happens, as is the case today, when one of many possible cultures comes to dominate the world and threatens to destroy all other cultural possibilities in its wake?" (Rioux and Crean 1980, 7–9, our translation). The pervasive cultural imperialism of the United States dominated Rioux's worries for his national community. In this, Rioux shared the concerns raised by George Grant in his influential *Lament for a Nation* (1965).

Cultural domination, in the guise of American cultural imperialism, clashes with social emancipation and undermines equality, leading Rioux and Crean to argue that "Our view is that today the collectivity that is richest in creative potential, the nation, is also that which is most threatened by imperialism" (1980, 11, our translation).

For Rioux, it was clear that the sovereignty-association project constituted a unique opportunity to maintain the richness of Canada's two national communities. Here is what he had to say at the time of the May 1980 referendum: "While it is perfectly understandable that partisans of sovereignty-association begin to convince Quebecers of the viability of their option, it is necessary to convince other Canadians that this type of rebuilding of Canada represents perhaps the last chance to save something of these two nations" (Rioux and Crean 1980, 8–9, our translation). Just as the differences between Québécois and other Canadians are increasingly well known, so the similarities between the two nations needs to be better understood and acknowledged. On this basis a true partnership could be built to better resist the common threat of Americanization.

The two-nations thesis is a constant in the work of Rioux, and it is through its political realization that he saw a solution to the political and cultural crisis facing Canada. Contrary to Charles Taylor who feels that symbolic recognition can satisfy Québécois, Rioux did not see how this could materialize without independence. It is only after each partner has recognized the other that it will be possible to achieve equality.

Rioux's socialism was co-equal with his nationalism, and he opposed any independence project that did nothing more than replace American and English Canadian capitalists with Quebec capitalists. He asserted that "This sort of nationalism can only lead to a sort of national liberation that propels into power a new set of political and economic elites" (Rioux and Crean 1980, 13, our translation). In short, such a changing of the guard would not improve social conditions for the majority of citizens. Rioux nurtured a desire to see people questioning their own society as they build their own national project of a kind that repudiates elite replacement.

It is the continued threat exercised by Americanization on their respective national projects that led Rioux and Crean to join forces to sensitize their fellow citizens. Quoting John Porter, Rioux reminded his readers that he shared his colleague's interpretation: "The best way to describe the main goal of Canadian society, writes John Porter, is to define it as an integrative objective. The maintenance of national unity has integrated or subsumed all other objectives ... As a consequence, the principal leaning of Canadian politics has been to the right; that of maintaining and preserving the status quo" (Rioux and Crean 1980, 27–8, our translation). This concern for national unity has contributed to the neglect of other issues, chief among them the question of cultural invasion, for both Québécois and other Canadians (Rioux 1990a, 253–4).

Equality cannot be achieved if economic or cultural domination is allowed. For Rioux, as for George Grant, cultural domination is the most devastating form of domination since there is little one can do to curtail it. "[Cultural hegemony] is the most insidious form of imperialism; it involves neither military occupation nor political and economic bullying, but rather the invasion of images, sounds, worlds and forms that portray a society of abundance and dreams" (Rioux and Crean 1980, 67, our translation). To escape this situation, Rioux invites Quebec and the rest of Canada to consider sovereignty-association in order to explore new avenues. "It is likely that once a new form of association is put in place the citizens of each of our nations will be more likely to appreciate their own worth and to collaborate ... No one wins if we allow for the maintenance of constitutional and political arrangements that were put in place for us rather than by us" (Rioux and Crean 1980, 114, our translation).

In his quest for greater equality, Rioux was concerned not only with nations but with regions. Reading through his works, one is immediately struck by Rioux's natural inclination to support those on the periphery of society, including regional peripheries. To paraphrase Rioux, if all regions [individuals] are equal in principle, some become more equal than others in practice (Rioux 1990c, 441). This line of thinking has remained constant throughout his entire life.

COMMUNITY

To complete our consideration of Rioux's philosophical trilogy, it is essential to turn our attention to the place of community. In our discussion of liberty and equality, it became clear that Rioux's thoughts on these matters acquire their full significance in the context of his ideas on community. Rioux maintained that liberty is best manifested through the expression of communal diversity and equality between all communities, from the smallest to the most inclusive.

The dynamic between individual and community is always present in Rioux's thinking. His interpretation has inspired many Québécois to come to terms with procedural and communitarian liberalism, though this is not often acknowledged in the literature. As early as 1957, Rioux stated: "In a socio-cultural order taken as a whole, the concept of society places emphasis on both the group of individuals composing this whole and their relationships with each other within it" (Rioux 1957, 78, our translation).

The place of the individual is key to understanding Rioux's conception of community. Rioux argued that Quebec, as a country, can be strong and dynamic only if each and every one of its citizens and collectivities feels like an integral and active participant in the project to build a new society – a society in which everyone can flourish in full diversity (Rioux 1977, 36).

In some writings, Rioux insisted on the need to establish stronger links with the Aboriginal peoples. Like his contemporaries, however,

Rioux gave only some attention to this central question. His interest in Aboriginal peoples was expressed early in his career (1951b, 1955b). He spoke of the need for Quebec to propose an inclusive social and national project in which they would be associated. Following the election of the Parti Québécois in 1976, he asserted:

> Taking seriously the idea that we want to build in Quebec a new society means developing this project in association with all Quebec's inhabitants, including the First Nations, Inuit and all other groups. We cannot afford to ignore the cultural richness of these groups, a richness that will contribute to making Quebec a land where everyone can fully and freely participate in the realization of a common ideal. (Rioux 1977, 36, our translation)

Rioux's quest for a just society led him to advocate self-management (*autogestion*) and to argue in favour of a devolution of powers towards regional, ethnic, cultural, and other collectivities (Rioux 1978b, 8–9). Throughout his writings, he maintained that national freedom was not to be achieved at the expense of the full expression of the regions or other communities. National freedom is about freeing all collectivities.

Being a libertarian, Rioux was also troubled by excessive state centralization. He was more inclined to trust individuals. In his quest for equality, he believed that emancipation "from below" was preferable to state interventions (1977, 34–6; 1978b, 1978–79; 1983; 1990b). He argued that the multidimensional nature of the problems associated with regional inequalities and uneven development could not be used to justify "the propensity within Quebec for bureaucratic centralization and long distance administration" (Rioux 1977, 34–5, our translation). For Rioux, regional autonomy was the spatial equivalent of self-management in the factories: an essential element of a free, equal, and self-governing society. National liberation for Quebec would not be achieved for the benefit of bureaucrats and technocrats. State expansion for its own sake was anathema to Rioux, who called for the devolution of state powers to regional and local organizations. The challenge for state managers was clear:

> to show enough fortitude to make themselves obsolete by passing on responsibilities to citizens' groups that wish to nurture their own creative projects founded on grassroots solidarity. This means that diversity of

classes, regions, and ethnic groups should be recognized within Quebec itself. Because of many decades of resistance, it was necessary to emphasize the community as a whole; but once our collective emancipation is realized we will have to initiate policies that recognize our internal diversity." (Rioux 1979, 208, our translation)

Rioux always presented a portrait of Quebec society that focussed on social pluralism and that called for a political space in which sovereignty is shared among individuals, communities, and regions. Concerned that capitalism, which he viewed as the freedom to exploit and oppress others, would destroy citizens, he sought to imagine alternatives. With Crean, he argued that individuals are not reducible to consumers. Moreover, when it came to social and cultural change, size mattered. Small nations "like ours," wrote Rioux and Crean, faced fewer obstacles, in the form of established interests, and therefore "could be audacious enough to imagine another type of life and society" (Rioux and Crean 1980, 110, our translation). As well, in an observation reminiscent of Harold Innis, it was those who were not the power-wielders, those on the margins of society, who harboured the most potential for imaginative change and exhibited the most dynamism when it came to breaking out of the oppressive constraints of the economic and social status quo (Rioux and Crean 1980, 111).

CONCLUSION

Always a voice for the exploited, the dominated, and the marginal, Marcel Rioux added his understanding of liberty, community, and equality to debates surrounding Quebec's quest for self-assertion in North America. As an anthropologist, Rioux consistently emphasized the value of small communities as the basis for the Good Life/Society, and maintained that power ought to emerge from below as opposed to being imposed from above. Operating from a sociological perspective, Rioux's interests were to be found at the level of community life, and it was in such activity that the pre-conditions for social solidarity would emerge.

For Rioux, nationalism could contribute to the advancement of progressive ideas, allowing for a 'new beginning' in Quebec that would permit new possibilities for communities and individuals. A constant theme that ran through his work was the denunciation of established dogma and ideological rigidity in any political and social project. Instead, any vision for Quebec society would do well to incorporate a sense in which all possibilities were left open – where communities could actively engage and contribute to the political process and change could be found in the everyday activities of the common citizen. National freedom meant freeing all collectivities in Quebec society, and this required devolution of powers to regional, ethnic, cultural, and other groups whose activities would contribute in the project to build a new society. For Rioux, the independence movement was a temporary facet of his broader vision – once collective emancipation for the community as a whole was achieved, the Quebec state could finally serve the ends of promoting internal diversity and nourish collective, self-managing initiatives by constituent groups. Nationalism and Quebec independence were simply vehicles through which a progressive society that promoted social pluralism could be crafted. Concerned with 'creeping Americanization' and individualism associated with the capitalist mainstream in North America, Rioux envisioned social and political equality as foundational principles for a new Quebec.

Underlying Rioux's views on liberty, equality, and community was a profound interest in culture, particularly cultural transcendence. Sovereignty would allow for somewhat of a *carte blanche* for Quebec, freeing it from dependence, constituting a genuinely self-governing society, and allowing for the construction of new cultural boundaries. Owing to his epistemological bias towards practice rather than theory, Rioux believed freedom involved the renewal and constant re-creation of cultural contexts. He stressed the limitless potential of human agency and was often at odds with many of his Marxist contemporaries who approached equality from a perspective of social determinism. For Rioux, equality could be the product of freedom – which he took to mean freedom to overcome alienation and social determinism; "men make their own history and create their own societies." He believed critical theory was incomplete unless it offered alternative visions for society, and in cultural development he saw the potential for the conquest of human possibilities – for ever more freedom. As such, Rioux believed that equality between national communities in Canada was at the very least a starting point for his much more ambitious visions for social emancipation. Tackling the issue of a subjugated Quebec in capitalist North America was thus a priority. In the end,

Rioux remained consistent in his appreciation for the boundless potential of human beings as agents of social emancipation and the interminable quest for social justice. This persistent theme rested on his eternal optimism that if allowed to act in a propitious political and social setting, the *possibilities* for humanity are endless.

CHAPTER SIX

The Communitarian Liberalism of Charles Taylor

Charles Taylor is, in the eyes of many, Canada's pre-eminent living philosopher. His international reputation was established through his work on Hegel and through numerous philosophical papers published in the 1970s and 1980s. More recently, Taylor has produced a sweeping analysis of the philosophical roots and contradictions of modern western thought in *Sources of the Self* and *The Malaise of Modernity* (published in the United States under the title, *The Ethics of Authenticity*). The erudition of his œuvre is staggering. His status as one of the pre-eminent thinkers in the Anglo-American world is undeniable.

Canadians, however, are more likely to know of Taylor in connection with his writings on Canadian politics and his activities within the political left. His book, *The Pattern of Politics*, was part of the "canon" of the nationalist left during the 1970s. Taylor's status as one of the major intellectual figures on the Canadian left had already been established through his contributions to *Cité libre* and *Canadian Dimension* during the 1960s when he was actively involved in the New Democratic Party as federal vice-president and also as an unsuccessful NDP candidate on four occasions (1962, 1963, 1965, 1968).

Taylor's early writings on Canadian politics dealt chiefly with a trio of issues: French-English relations, social and economic justice, and American influence on Canadian economics, culture, and politics. The emphases in his more recent work on Canada have shifted somewhat. French-English relations, including such related matters as Quebec nationalism, national unity, and the constitution, continue to be among Taylor's main concerns. But the earlier emphases on American imperialism and social and economic justice have been pushed aside by multiculturalism and the problem of retrieving and nurturing a sense of community in liberal-capitalist societies.

While no single label does justice to Taylor's sophisticated and wide-ranging œuvre, the dominant theme in his writings is how to balance freedom and community. Taylor is usually considered to be a prominent contemporary communitarian, but this characterization fails to acknowledge the strong liberalism that runs throughout his work. We prefer to call Taylor a liberal-communitarian, on the grounds that it is the tension between individual freedom and communal goods that lies at the heart of his political philosophy and is its distinguishing characteristic. Like Trudeau, Taylor's background as a bilingual Quebecer who has lived most of his life in Montreal makes him especially sensitive to the competing claims of individual and group rights and the different visions of the good that follow from emphasizing one or the other.

Parochial is the last word that would describe Taylor's thought. Nevertheless, there are recognizably Canadian concerns and modes of thinking that surface even when his subject is not Canada per se. Taylor's anti-Americanism – over which Canadians do not hold a monopoly, but are surely among the world's most adept and experienced practitioners – is firmly in the tradition of the Canadian left. His defense of state intervention to promote communal goods like regional development, his antipathy toward individualistic philosophies, his sympathy for nationalist aspirations, and his support for multiculturalism and the rights of Aboriginal peoples are all familiar strands in the tapestry of Canadian politics. It would be absurd to argue that Taylor's philosophy has been shaped in some deterministic way by his Canadian background. On the other hand, these influences are not absent from his work, as we will show in the following pages.

FREEDOM

Charles Taylor is known to be a staunch critic of liberal politics, capitalist economics, and individualistic – he would say "atomistic" –

societies. It may seem odd, therefore, to begin an analysis of his political thought with the subject of freedom. In fact, however, Taylor's understanding of freedom is fundamental to his political philosophy. This may not be obvious to those who have read only his writings on Canadian politics. But questions of what freedom involves and what social arrangements best protect it are never far from the surface of his work, as is apparent in his more general philosophical writings.

There are two key aspects of Taylor's conception of freedom. First, *freedom is a social good*. It is only possible within society and therefore in association with other individuals. Second, *freedom is a moral good*. It does not involve being able to do whatever one desires. Rather, some choices are qualitatively superior to others, in the sense that they involve the exercise of real free will and fulfill the conditions of being a truly human subject. Other choices do not.

The roots of Taylor's ideas on freedom are found chiefly in the writings of Jean-Jacques Rousseau and Immanuel Kant. He is dismissive of individualistic primacy-of-rights theories whose origins lie in the liberal philosophy of Thomas Hobbes and John Locke. Rousseau and Kant, Taylor argues, develop a positive notion of freedom that relies on a moral conception of the human being in society. Hobbes and Locke, on the other hand, offer a negative conception of liberty – freedom as the absence of constraint – that is amoral and that collapses under the weight of its logical and practical contradictions.

What Taylor finds most objectionable in the negative conception of freedom is its refusal to judge the goodness of the choices individuals make. Freedom, he argues, cannot be considered apart from ethics. This is precisely what the advocates of negative liberty do, however, when they refuse to make qualitative distinctions between different life plans and actions, arguing instead that the individual is the only fair judge of what will promote or impair his or her happiness, satisfaction, etc. They place individual rights before all else and build their social and political theories on the primacy of these rights and the derivative nature of social obligations. Such theories, Taylor argues, conceive of society as a rather unfortunate but necessary encumbrance that limits the human ability to be free.

The truth, says Taylor, is wholly opposite. He maintains that the notion of rights presupposes certain human capacities that are considered worthy, and that these capacities can only be developed and nurtured in society, so that the idea of the primacy of rights is incoherent. In a critique of what he calls the "atomistic" philosophies of individual rights descended from Hobbes, Taylor sets forth what he believes are the social conditions of freedom:

> [D]eveloped freedom requires a certain understanding of self, one in which the aspirations to autonomy and self-direction become conceivable; and second, that this self-understanding is not something we can sustain on our own, but that our identity is always partly defined in conversation with others or through the common understanding which underlies the practices of our society. The thesis is that the identity of the autonomous, self-determining individual requires a social matrix, one for instance which through a series of practices recognizes the right to autonomous decision and which calls for the individual having a voice in deliberation about public action. (1985c, 198)

Taylor's argument that individual freedom is only possible in society, and, moreover, in a particular sort of society, is based on two more fundamental premises. One involves his dialogical understanding of individual identity. Following Erik Erikson, he argues that one acquires an identity and experiences personal meaning through one's relations to significant others including family, society, and God (1970, 103ff). This continues throughout one's life, so that the problem of individual identity, including that of individual freedom, is inseparable from the conditions of community existence. All important personal meanings are generated through communal attachments, including what it means to be free. Indeed, the decline in the opportunities to affirm and experience public meanings has contributed to the crisis of personal identity which is at the heart of what Taylor calls the malaise of modernity.

But the second premise underlying Taylor's social conception of freedom is equally crucial. Following Rousseau, he insists on the importance of the quality of motivation. Like Rousseau, he argues that actions which do not accord with what are truly significant purposes, i.e. purposes that relate to what is distinctive about the human condition, are not evidence of free will. "Freedom is important to us," he writes, "because we are purposive beings. But then there must be distinctions in the significance of different kinds of freedom based on the distinction in the significance of different purposes" (1985d, 219). Properly understood, therefore, freedom is not the ability to do what I like free from external constraint, but is rather the capacity to respond to and act in ways consonant with inner freedom. "I must be actually exercising self-understanding in order to be truly or fully free," says Taylor. "I can no longer understand freedom just as an opportunity-concept" (1985d, 229).

Taylor's conception of freedom as an inner quality that connects the individual to society draws on Rousseau and Kant. Following Rousseau, he argues that the mere fact of having chosen my path does not make it good and me free. My choices must accord with my true sentiments, with the voice of nature/reason as this is expressed through me. This is what personal authenticity and individual freedom are truly about. They are linked to an idea of the good life that is attainable through human reason, and which can only be achieved in the society of others.

Taylor rejects the "unhooking of freedom from any link with the idea of a moral order ... according to which good and bad conduct are no longer distinguished by the motivation which inspires each" (1985f, 319). Acting freely involves acting virtuously, where one's behaviour accords with moral principles. Here Taylor follows Kant:

> If to be free is to follow the moral law, and to act morally is to see that the maxim of my action could be willed universally, then freedom requires that I understand myself as standing under a law that applies as well to others, one that is not addressed to me alone, but to rational subjects as such. So being free is standing in a certain kind of moral order... ("Kant's Theory of Freedom," 1985f, 326)

society?

So individual freedom requires society, and not just any form of society but one structured along the lines of Kant's categorical imperative. This brings us back to Taylor's argument that individual freedom can only be maintained in a society of a certain sort. Consequently, the individual has a responsibility to preserve this society. But what sort of society makes possible individual freedom? Taylor is quite certain that it is not the sort of individualistic society represented by the United States, where relatively great inequalities in wealth and living conditions are tolerated on the ostensible grounds that this is in fact the price of freedom. Nor is it any manner of laissez-faire market economy whose priorities, he argues, are socially irrational (1970: 30–31). Public institutions, including economic ones, that permit too great inequalities must end up denying real freedom to many who are cut off from the conditions needed to behave as distinctively human agents and, thus, as free individuals. The positive state is necessary for the promotion and protection of freedom, and not simply to ensure a more just distribution of wealth, opportunities, and recognition in society.

Taylor's conception of freedom is not without its problems. Even if one accepts his argument that freedom matters because we are purposive beings, and that we cannot and in practice do not avoid judging the goodness of the choices people make, it is still not clear on what grounds these judgments are to be made. Taylor is somewhat vague on this point, although one has a sense that he would agree with Tocqueville that,

> Mankind is subject to general and permanent wants that have created moral laws, to the neglect of which men have ever and in all places attached the notion of censure and shame: to infringe them was *to do ill; to do well* was to conform to them. (Tocqueville 1994, 230)

Moreover, Taylor would doubtless agree with Tocqueville that individualism "at first only saps the virtues of public life; but in the long run it attacks and destroys all others and is at length absorbed in downright selfishness" (Tocqueville 1994, 98). An individualistic democracy, says Tocqueville, "throws [man] back forever upon himself alone and threatens in the end to confine him entirely within the solitude of his own heart" (Tocqueville 1994, 99).

Tocqueville is one of the writers whom Taylor often cites approvingly. The general and permanent wants that have created "moral laws" of which Tocqueville speaks correspond to Taylor's notion of the distinctively human qualities that are affirmed through free will. We are not much further ahead, however, in knowing what these are. But in *Sources of the Self* and *The Malaise of Modernity*, Taylor identifies *authenticity* – self-determining freedom that is exercised against moral horizons linking the individual to the community – as the measure against which actions may be judged. "Moral horizons" are critical to what Taylor has in mind. He is quite certain that authenticity, or what Rousseau called "le sentiment de l'existence," can only be achieved when an individual recognizes his connection to a wider whole. This brings us to the edge of Taylor's conception of community which, as we shall see, flows from his particular notion of what it is to be free.

We are not left, however, without any guide as to how Taylor would determine whether a choice conforms to self-determining freedom, and is therefore both an expression of personal authenticity and morally good. Throughout his writings there runs a criticism of individualistic ("atomistic," he would say) liberal-capitalist societies that are based on a negative conception of liberty. Real freedom, Taylor argues, is achieved and nurtured through collective enterprises that, far from limiting the individual's freedom, make freedom possible by linking individual choices and actions to the broader purposes that make us genuinely human. Do all collective endeavours promote freedom? Neither Taylor nor any other prominent communitarian would go this far. But Taylor's insistence on the social aspects of the individual and the need for communal attachments in order to achieve the state of authenticity that is so central to the post-Romantic age place him on the side of the social-welfare state, greater redistribution of wealth, and other forms of state intervention that liberals believe threaten freedom.

EQUALITY

Equality was the central issue addressed in Taylor's early work, particularly *The Pattern of Politics*. That book was a sort of manifesto of the Canadian left, attacking what Taylor called liberalism's consensus view of politics. It was a root-and-branch attack on market economics, individualist culture, mainstream consensus politics, and American influence. None of this was particularly original, but Taylor placed his personal mark on what otherwise would have been a fairly orthodox left-wing broadside through linking the objects of his attack to broader characteristics of modernity that would occupy him throughout his life.

The Pattern of Politics was written in what might be called the "angry young man" key. It was scholarly but at the same time polemical. It dealt directly with public policies instead of coming at them on the more abstract wavelength of the philosopher. Indeed, the book ended with a sweeping reform agenda implying that just about everything was broken and needed to be fixed. Perhaps disillusioned by the defeat of the Waffle candidate James Laxer at the NDP's 1971 leadership convention, and the movement's subsequent expulsion from the party, Taylor never again produced this sort of work. His œuvre has been devoted almost entirely to grander philosophical matters, but Taylor's early concern with equality has not been jettisoned. Instead, it has undergone a transmutation and surfaces in his discussion of such matters as community, multiculturalism, and nationalism.

There is nothing in Taylor's post-1970 work to suggest that he has abandoned the views he held as an angry young man of the Canadian political left. We will begin, therefore, with his ideas in *The Pattern of Politics*. Taylor's egalitarian politics is built on four main pillars. They include his critique of capitalism, alienation, anti-Americanism, and the loss of community. This last theme is, of course, the lens through which his more recent work views equality.

Taylor's dislike of capitalist economics is at the heart of his egalitarianism. He prefers the label "the corporate system" to capitalism or market economics, a preference that was shared during the 1960s by anti-establishment critics ranging from J.K. Galbraith on the liberal left to socialists like Michael Harrington and C. Wright Mills. The "corporate system" better captured the scope of capitalism's influence, signalling that it was not merely a set of economic arrangements but a system of power whose influence extended into social, cultural, and political realms. The corporate system generated massive inequalities in economic well-being and influence, but also in these other realms.

The problem with capitalist economics, according to Taylor, assumes two main forms. First, it inevitably leads to monopoly control over production, investment, and pricing decisions, whereby economic decision-making is concentrated in fewer and fewer hands and competition is effectively abolished in the chief sectors of the economy. This argument had been popularized by J.K. Galbraith whose work is cited approvingly by Taylor (1970, 17–19). (Taylor is not the only prominent Canadian thinker to admire Galbraith's work. Pierre Trudeau was also impressed and, as prime minister, had the opportunity to implement some of Galbraith's ideas.) Second, capitalism is inefficient, thus failing to deliver on its major and least questioned claim. Taylor writes,

> ... the bent of the corporate system is towards the production of goods and services for individual consumption. But the system tends to resist

increased production of those goods and services that have to be provided collectively. (1970, 28)

Later he adds that "Everyone knows that the balance between public and private investment in our society is all wrong" (1970, 31).

One is reminded here of the title of Galbraith's left-liberal call to arms, *Private Affluence and Public Squalor.* Taylor refers to the "mad priorities" of the corporate system (1970, 31) which most politicians do not care to challenge for ideological reasons, but which even reformist governments find difficult to counter because of "the corporate system's power of *riposte*, the power of withholding capital with all that this entails" (1970, 32). And so society invests its scarce resources in the development of new – and largely unnecessary – consumer appliances rather than in public education, assistance for those in need, and protection of the environment.

The corporate system's pernicious consequences are not, however, limited to these. They include debased social values promoted through advertising, and the materialist culture of consumption that the corporate system depends on to keep running. Moreover, the system of production that exists under capitalism alienates workers from themselves and what they produce, as Marx argued. We will return to Taylor's ideas on alienation later in this chapter.

The reverse side of Taylor's critique of the corporate system is his advocacy of *dirigiste* economics. The reform program he set forth in the final chapter of *The Pattern of Politics* was unexceptional left-wing fare, advocating large doses of economic planning, vastly greater investment in public goods like education and social services, channelling of economic resources into economically backward regions, and the patriation of much foreign-owned capital. A huge public investment fund would be the chief vehicle for implementing the economic-planning agenda Taylor envisaged. His evident faith in *dirigisme* shows up in the curiously lavish praise he heaps on Italy's policies to promote economic development in that country's mezzogiorno regions (curious because, even when Taylor was writing, the economic gap between the north and south of Italy was enormous, and skepticism regarding the long-term effectiveness of regional investment policies was pretty general, except among those committed to such redistribution for ideological reasons) (1970, 42, 141). He also draws unfavourable comparisons between "the different norms of corporate autonomy accepted in Europe and those in the Anglo-Saxon world, particularly North America" (1970, 26), and laments that free enterprise ideology "seems to be a peculiarly English-speaking invention" (see footnote 1970, 27).

All of this is perfectly consistent with Taylor's view that capitalist economics is inefficient and pernicious from the standpoint of society. The best he can say for what the existing economic system produces is that "Ours is an advanced country, which means principally that the proportion of our population which we will allow to fester in poverty is much less than fifty percent (1970, 84). This is clearly the voice of Taylor the "angry young man." Others would argue that market economics, for all its faults and inequities, produces a level of affluence for the vast majority that is beyond what any other set of economic arrangements has achieved: the venerable, if not uncontested, greatest good for the greatest number argument. What attracts his attention and his ire are the undeniable inequalities produced under capitalism.

Taylor's preoccupation with the huge differences in wealth and economic influence that capitalism permits also leads him to neglect the putative salutory consequences of private property ownership. That he ignores the possible economic benefits accepted by Adam Smith's followers as articles of faith is not surprising given his view that collectivized decision-making produces economic choices that are more rational for society than the cumulative results of private decision-making. That he is unconvinced by arguments that private property ownership may be an important, even crucial, bulwark of individual freedom is perhaps more surprising, until one understands Taylor's conception of freedom. As we explained in the previous section of this chapter, his social conception of freedom could probably accommodate the communal ownership of most property without this being seen to jeopardize individual liberty.

A second pillar of Taylor's egalitarian political philosophy involves alienation. This is a subject that is central to much of his recent work on modernity and the loss of community, but in fact reaches back to *The Pattern of Politics*. While the alienation of the individual in atomistic society was already a concern of Taylor's, he also had much to say about the alienation of false consciousness. By this is meant the double failure of most people to perceive their real class interests and of party politics to be structured on class lines. Taylor, like virtually all Canadian leftists of his generation, was highly critical of what he called liberalism's consensus model of politics, and called for its replacement by a politics of polarization – "creative politics" as reformers often called it – that would recognize the primary importance of class identification and conflict.

The alienation of false consciousness clearly has to do with equality. "[C]onsensus politics," Taylor writes, "hinge on the relative ignorance or mystification of those in a society who are most disadvantaged by it. It thrives at their expense" (1970, 5). The mass of people are duped, taken in by a system that hides from them the sorts of economic, social, and political arrangements that would best promote their true well-being and happiness. The dominant political parties and the privately owned, advertising-dependent media promote this false consciousness, but perhaps the chief cause involves the values associated with a mass consumption society. Where the quantity of consumer goods becomes the chief standard for evaluating individual and social well-being and measuring progress, individuals will increasingly experience a sort of "'privatization,' that is, the tendency for people to find meaning for their lives on their own outside of the collectively celebrated public meanings" (1970, 57). Collective enterprises and communal attachments are starved of nourishment where the consumer-goods standard rules. This cult of the Gross National Product is accompanied by what Taylor calls "machine fetishism," where "our rhythm and, in part, our form of life [are] moulded by the demands of a changing technology," to the detriment of truly human priorities (1970, 58–9). Together, the cult of the GNP and machine fetishism reinforce the myth of the corporate system's superior efficiency; the myth of its ability to deliver the goods (more goods! better goods!) and in the process produce the greatest sum of human happiness.

In fact, says Taylor, the dominant value system of modern capitalism and the politics of consensus which is its handmaiden serve to reinforce inequality in society. They mask its reality and fail to give it a voice because of their refusal to acknowledge that a significant minority of the population is excluded from the affluent society. The alienation of false consciousness stands in the way of political identifications and alliances, ways of thinking and believing in politics, that would challenge the domination of the corporate system.

Anti-Americanism is a third pillar of Taylor's politics of equality. There are echoes of George Grant's *Lament for a Nation* and *Technology and Empire* in his early writings, although in a distinctively left-wing key. Anti-Americanism has long been, of course, *de rigueur* on the Canadian left. Taylor partakes in this anti-Americanism on two levels: that of what might be called the soul-destroying qualities of American influence (Taylor does not use this term, but one suspects that he would not object to it) and, second, that country's impact on Canada's ability to make its own economic and political choices and, ultimately, generate a more just society than that of the United States. The second of these levels concerns us now.

In *The Pattern of Politics* Taylor draws heavily on Kari Levitt's *Silent Surrender* in explaining what he argues to be the pernicious consequences of American ownership in Canada. Instead of enriching Canada, as is commonly assumed, Taylor argues that foreign ownership actually impoverishes the country. Ultimately, he says, those who suffer most are the poor and the working class, through the inefficent allocation of investment dictated by American capital, and the political unwillingness to tax foreign-owned corporations at a fair rate for fear of driving away what is wrongly believed to be the capital and entrepreneurial talent that is not available domestically.

Taylor argues that market ideology serves to insulate American ownership from criticism. "Since the major corporations are all almost exclusively American," he writes, "it is impossible to challenge American control of our economy without running the risk of impiety" (1970, 95). Nationalist policies and economic planning are the only means of asserting control over Canada's economic and political destiny. This independence is, according to Taylor, good in itself. But it is even more important because of the redistributive possibilities it opens up. The nationalist option would "give us the means to make the increased independence worthwhile; for we would have the planning structures necessary to achieve our major social goals, such as regional development" (1970, 94).

The fourth pillar of Taylor's egalitarian politics, and the most distinctive element in his thinking about equality, involves the loss of community. In *The Pattern of Politics* he began to sketch the implications for equality of what he called the atrophy of public meanings in industrial society. Beginning from his view that human beings are creatures who seek meaning in purposes that connect them to others, Taylor argues that this need is increasingly denied by the privatization of experience that conditions in industrial society – capitalist *and* communist – generate. The loss of common purposes, which is a symptom of privatization, undermines equality by starving the public realm through which these purposes could be pursued. What is left, he argues, is just not enough to maintain human dignity:

> One can, of course, exult in the existence of a society whose basic idea is the primacy of the private purpose. This is in a sense what we see in the United States. But, by itself, private purpose is too thin an idea to call for full-hearted celebration, and its real power today lies in its role in American nationalism – the celebration of the greatness of America as a just reward for the rightness of a way of life. (1970, 106)

The anti-government theme that has deep roots in the American political tradition serves to undermine equality by enfeebling the state, the necessary locus for the definition and direction of public meanings and purposes which Taylor argues are essential to the achievement of the good life. Where the state is viewed in purely instrumental terms, as merely a "service institution" (1993, 127) that has no essential role to play in our collective self-definition, not only is national unity compromised, so too is the possibility of achieving collective goals that promote the dignity of all and a greater degree of equality than is possible under American-style institutions and cultural norms. Taylor points to the Canadian tradition of state intervention stretching from the Canadian Pacific Railway to Medicare and the National Energy Policy as proof of what he claims is Canada's more communal democratic political culture, based on a stronger identification of individuals with the fate of the community than one finds in the United States (1993, 95–7).

As an aside, Taylor's ability to cite the CPR and NEP as proofs of Canadians' superior sense of community and willingness to use the state to advance communal goals betrays an insensitivity to western Canadian perspectives on these institutions and policies. Far from being considered shining beacons of Canadians' community-mindedness they are more likely to be viewed by westerners as symbols of eastern Canada's domination of this country's politics and that region's eagerness to sacrifice western interests to those of the Ontario-Quebec axis. But Taylor, like Trudeau, has almost nothing to say about the concerns and distinctive cultural norms of the West.

COMMUNITY

Since Taylor is a leading member of the communitarian school within contemporary philosophy, it may seem odd to leave a discussion of his thoughts on community to the latter part of this chapter. We have done so deliberately, however, in order to show that his communitarianism is built on a foundation of premises and arguments about freedom and equality. Nonetheless, his recent writings have placed the problems of community and identity – inextricably related matters in Taylor's thought – at centre stage. As he writes in *Sources of the Self*, his goal is one of "retrieval." What he attempts to retrieve is the Romantic notion of human freedom and personal identity that are in harmony with, and have their wellsprings in, a sense of community.

In order to understand Taylor's conception of community and its importance in human affairs, we must return to his thoughts on the human condition. As we noted in discussing Taylor's theory of freedom, his fundamental premise is the social nature of the human being. By this he does not mean the obvious fact that men and women need one another in order to procreate, and that some amount of cooperation between individuals renders life less "nasty, brutish and short," as Hobbes put it. Instead, Taylor means that the social dimension of the human condition is at the heart of what it is to be a fully human subject. Our identity, our sense of self, and the realization of a good life (Taylor does not call it a virtuous life, but this clearly is what he has in mind) are dependent on our relationships to others. The human being in the mythical state of nature is not simply an historical impossibility, but is not even human. To be a truly human subject requires the presence, physical or otherwise, of others.

The basis of Taylor's communitarian vision is ontological. He insists on what he calls the *dialogical* character of human life as the crucial factor shaping our consciousness and identity. "We define our identity always in dialogue with, sometimes in struggle against, the things our significant others want to see in us," Taylor writes. He adds that "Even after we outgrow some of these others – our parents, for instance – and they disappear from our lives, the conversation with them continues within us as long as we live" (1992, 33). By itself, this insistence on the vital influence of the "other" on the development of an individual's sense of self is an unremarkable commonplace of modern psychology. It becomes, however, the linchpin in Taylor's communitarian politics through the connections he establishes between dialogically determined identity, authenticity, and ethics.

By authenticity Taylor means being true to ourselves, to our own uniqueness; experiencing what Rousseau called *le sentiment de l'existence*. Following Rousseau, he maintains that authenticity can only be achieved when our sentiments "connect us to a wider whole ... [During] the Romantic period the self-feeling and the feeling of belonging to nature were linked. Perhaps the loss of a sense of belonging through a publicly defined order needs to be compensated by a stronger, more inner sense of linkage" (1991, 91). In pre-modern times what Rousseau called the *sentiment de l'existence* was unproblematic. Socially derived identities and the sense of connection between the individual and the community were built into the social categories that generally were taken for granted and that structured the lives of individuals. But in modern societies, where the externally generated sources of communal association are much weaker, self-making becomes problematic. The desacralization of life and the breakdown of the traditional modalities through which one's sense of self was formed opened the doors to the problem of authenticity and how to achieve it.

The dilemma of modern people is that they seek authenticity in a world that provides fewer and fewer opportunities to satisfy this craving. It is not enough to be able to "do your own thing." Authenticity involves being true to oneself in a way that connects the individual to a wider whole and integrates the subject into the human community. But why? Taylor's answer exposes the degree to which his philosophy is underpinned by a communitarian notion of virtue. In The *Malaise of Modernity* Taylor argues that,

> ... unless some options are more significant than others, the very idea of self-choice falls into triviality and hence incoherence. Self-choice as an ideal makes sense only because some issues are more significant than others ... The ideal couldn't stand alone, because it requires a horizon of issues of importance, which help define the *respects* in which self-making is significant. (1991, 39)

The notion of a "horizon of issues of importance" introduces an ethical standard into the attempt to achieve authenticity. Taylor is quite certain that this necessary horizon is not provided by contemporary liberalism which, he argues, can only come up with an individual's own happiness or satisfaction as a benchmark, and so reinforces separation. It is precisely their sense of being walled up within themselves that needs to be overcome if men and women are to experience true freedom and achieve their longing for *le sentiment de l'existence.* In *The Sources of the Self* Taylor devotes several chapters to a discussion of post-Enlightenment art and literature, in order to show that the craving for authenticity through reestablished bonds of community is a central dilemma today.

We may summarize the discussion to this point of Taylor's communitarianism by saying that an individual's identity is created dialogically. In the modern age this identity is linked to the achievement of a sense of authenticity, realizing one's uniqueness. This may only be accomplished, however, through experiencing a sense of connection to a wider whole. Thus, individual identity and authenticity depend upon a sense of community. Finally, the search for authenticity has ethical implications because of the unavoidability of a horizon of issues of importance against which choices may be judged.

This matter of a moral horizon leads to the question of dignity. This is a central concept in Taylor's thought, and is necessary to an understanding of his arguments about nationalism and the recognition of group identities. The moral horizon that enables us to achieve the sense of connection to a wider whole that Taylor argues is essential to authenticity is one that recognizes the equal dignity of all. Like Rousseau, Taylor rejects those forms of honour and dignity that rely on special preference. He maintains that dignity must rest on equality, reciprocity, and unity of purpose. Taylor writes,

> This unity makes possible the equality of esteem, but the fact that esteem is in principle equal in this system is essential to the unity of purpose itself. Under the aegis of the general will, all virtuous citizens are to be equally honored. The age of dignity is born. (1992, 49)

But what is this unity of purpose to which Taylor refers? It seems to be a presumption of equal worth that one ought to make in responding to others and other cultures. In the republic of virtuous citizens all men and women are assumed to be of equal worth, and therefore to possess dignity in equal measure. Dignity rests, therefore, on equality and tolerance. This should not be confused, however, with a sort of soft moral relativism that refuses to discriminate between the virtuousness of different individuals and the comparative worth of different cultures. But it does provide a basis for Taylor's defense of public recognition for group identities.

It seems that passive toleration is not enough to support the politics of equal dignity. To understand why not we need to recall Taylor's initial premise about individual identity being dialogically determined. It is shaped through the continuous encounters that take place between an individual and significant others throughout one's life. Refusal on the part of others to recognize those characteristics which a person believes to be central to personal identity may not amount to active discrimination, but nonetheless denies the equal dignity of the person whose identity is not affirmed. This, Taylor argues, is what is at stake when Québécois demand recognition of special status for their province and anglophone Canadians reject their demand. He writes,

> When this kind of denial takes place, or seems to do so in the eyes of a minority group, it is hard and sometimes impossible for the members of that minority group to feel that they are really being given an equal hearing; for what they stand for seems to be at best invisible and perhaps actively rejected by the majority, and thus cannot count with them. In effect, what pertains to the minority identity is not being given a hearing. In this way, a prolonged refusal of recognition between groups in a society can erode the common understanding of equal participation on which a functioning liberal democracy crucially depends. Canada is a tragic case in point. (1992, 190)

Group identities, Taylor believes, are more than ever crucial in the modern age as a means of satisfying the natural human craving for a sense of connection to a wider whole. Community provides an anchor for individual identity. The universalistic standards of liberalism not only fail to satisfy this need, they produce subtle forms of discrimination while claiming to treat everyone equally. Taylor, however, endorses the argument that the achievement of real equality, as opposed to that of a merely formal sort, may require that the members of different groups be treated differently. Their communal identities must be accorded formal recognition and their distinctive conditions acknowledged.

And if they are not? The consequences are a denial of the equal dignity that people have a right to expect, a loss of self-esteem, and discrimination. "The projection of an inferior or demeaning image on another can actually distort and oppress, to the extent that the image is internalized," says Taylor. He adds that "*the withholding of recognition can be a form of oppression* ... [of] other-induced distortions" (emphasis added; 1992, 36–7). The refusal of English Canada to recognize Quebec as a distinct society is, Taylor argues, precisely this sort of oppression.

The most powerful identity in modern times is, of course, nationalism. As one would expect, Taylor is sympathetic to nationalist demands, at least to the extent that they are inspired by and seek to achieve a sense of communal identity that does not threaten the equal dignity owed to those who are not members of the nation. He recognizes, of course, that nationalism has often degenerated into various forms of xenophobia, intolerance, and aggression against those who are not part of the nation. But the impulse that gives rise to nationalism is, Taylor argues, unavoidable in the modern world and may be harnessed so as to produce sentiments of belonging and dignity that are crucial to the realization of one's identity. In answering the distinctively modern question "Who am I?" it is not at all surprising that people turn to that community to which they are tied by ethnic roots, culture, and language.

The universalism of liberal theory fails to acknowledge the importance, indeed the indispensability not merely in some social-psychological sense but in terms of realizing a life of authenticity and freedom, of national differences. Taylor writes,

> For each individual to discover in himself what his humanity consists in, he needs a horizon of meaning, which can only be provided by some allegiance, group membership, cultural tradition. He needs, in the broadest sense, a language in which to ask and answer the questions of ultimate significance ... Since the Romantic insight is that we need a language in the broadest sense in order to discover our humanity, and that this language is something we have access to through our community, it is natural that the community defined by natural language should become one of the most important poles of identification [for modern people]. (1992, 46, 47)

The search for authenticity, Taylor observes, involves an attempt to discover one's fundamental purposes and thereby forge a self-identity, autonomously. In the age of emancipation these purposes and this self-identity cannot be assumed, but must be discovered in oneself, a task which requires some horizon of meaning. "Nationalism," Taylor argues, "the singling out of linguistic nationality as the paradigm pole of self-identity, is part of this modern drive to emancipation" (1992, 47). It provides this "horizon of meaning." Moreover, nationalism of this benign sort is consonant with both individual self-rule and collective self-determination. These, Taylor avers, are good things.

Does all of this mean that nations as Taylor defines them, i.e., communities where people speak the same language, share a common history, and, of crucial importance, share a communal identification around these facts, must become states in order to realize the conditions of individual freedom/authenticity and collective self-determination? Not necessarily. What is essential is that opportunities for expression and realization in the language of one's national community be open in public life, not simply through the state but in economic life, the educational system, the arts, and all that is considered prestigious in modern society. But even this is not quite enough. It is also necessary that one's national identity be recognized, not merely tolerated, by others. This recognition is crucial to the self-respect of a nation, and explains why nationalists generally believe that nothing short of political sovereignty can enable them to experience fully their national identity. Though often portrayed as the self-serving demands of nationalist elites who would like a bigger, fancier stage on which to strut, the insistence on international recognition of the nation derives, Taylor maintains, from the dialogical character of identity formation. Both individuals and nations depend on others for their sense of self. Sovereignty that is recognized by other states provides the affirmation of collective identity that the members of a nation need.

Although a nationalist, Taylor is not a sovereignist. He believes that national expression, realization, and recognition are attainable within a framework that stops short of political sovereignty. In the case of Canada this would involve a form of federalism that accommodates Québécois demands for recognition through constitutional special status. Taylor quite rightly acknowledges that the province already has a sort of de facto special status by virtue of arrangements worked out between Quebec and Ottawa since the 1960s (e.g., opting out of some federal-provincial programs; occupying jurisdictional turf, as in the case of most immigration selection and acculturation services, that Ottawa controls for the rest of Canada; operating an elaborate international network of cultural offices). What is missing, however, is some formal recognition by the rest of Canada of the Québécois as a nation, recognition that English Canadians have shown themselves to be unwilling to extend in twice rejecting constitutional amendments that would have entrenched in the Constitution Quebec's status as a "distinct society."

Taylor recognizes that modern nationalism, including Québécois nationalism since the 1960s, may be a cloak for the interests of an upwardly mobile middle class and intelligentsia. Indeed, in his 1965 article, "Nationalism and the Political Intelligentsia," he makes a case quite similar to that which had already been made by Hubert Guindon and Albert Breton. The new nationalism of French-speaking Quebec was, they argued, a product of social and economic developments that created a new class of highly educated francophones whose professional training was in fields like engineering, communications, social sciences, management, and public administration. The ideological commitment of the traditional nationalism to pre-industrial values and the domination of the economy by anglophones served to block their aspirations. In order to overcome these obstacles the new intelligentsia/middle class turned to the Quebec state as the vehicle for achieving their goals. This is a story that has been told many times.

Taylor warns, however, that "it would be a mistake to give too rationalist and utilitarian a model of explanation to the rise and continuance of French-Canadian nationalism" (1992, 13). This is where he parts profoundly with the analysis of those such as Breton and Guindon, and also Trudeau. The utilitarian model portrays nationalism in a rather unflattering light as a self-interested project that provides benefits to the upwardly mobile middle class at the expense of those who occupy lower rungs on the socio-economic ladder. This interpretation, Taylor insists, does not acknowledge the crucial place of identity in generating and maintaining nationalist sentiment. Nationalism is not simply, or even chiefly, a matter of wanting a fair share of the jobs. It is about respect and achieving the conditions that enable members of a national community to see the value of their culture affirmed in the equal recognition accorded it by others. Nationalism is, after all, Taylor would say, about dignity.

That is why, he argues, the rejection of the Meech Lake Accord by English Canada was experienced by the Québécois as a serious affront, as a blow to their dignity. Although supporters of the Accord inside and outside Quebec stoutly insisted that its recognition of Quebec as a "distinct society" would neither add nor subtract from the powers of any government in Canada, they nevertheless maintained that distinct society status was not negotiable. Its importance lay in the sense of dignity that it would confer on Québécois. The primary issue was, therefore, one of respect and recognition, a fact that generally was obscured by all the talk about jurisdictional matters and legislative powers, and Quebec nationalists' ego-protecting denials that distinct society status mattered.

Is there a way out of the impasse that, in recent decades, has threatened to break up Canada? Taylor argues that the solution must come from the recognition of what he calls *deep diversity*. This involves a form of cultural pluralism that goes beyond the familiar liberal formula of respect for group differences under the rubric of a uniform citizenship that carries identical rights and obligations for all. Deep diversity achieves a sense of communal solidarity through permitting "a plurality of ways of belonging [to] be acknowledged and accepted" (1992, 183). To put it more concretely, one's attachment to a country like Canada would be experienced at one remove, through the fact that Canada represents a common identity pole for, say, Québécois, Cree, Dene, and communities in English Canada, each of which can belong to Canada in a different way.

Initially his rather vague recipe for deep diversity seems reminiscent of Joe Clark's "community of communities" formula. How can such vague conceptions really sustain a country? Taylor argues, however, that the deep diversity alternative has history on its side.

The uniform model of citizenship found in its classic form in countries like the United States and France has become passé, he maintains, increasingly ill-suited to the needs and demands of many modern societies.

> To be a citizen of a democratic society [according to this model] "is to be an individual with certain rights and duties among other individuals equally endowed. The citizen also belongs to other communities, familial, religious, ideological, built on tradition or affinity. But that is a matter for the private sphere. The state deals only with individuals, to which it accords rights and on which it makes claims. (1992, 198)

This model of citizenship may have seen its day, Taylor believes. International migration is changing the face of even those societies, like the United States and France, that pioneered and still champion the uniform citizenship model. The human craving for meaning and dignity through communal membership has fueled the politics of recognition. In these circumstances the classic liberal model of citizenship and political community fails to satisfy an increasing number of people. This, Taylor argues, is precisely the predicament Canada faces.

There are, he believes, two options. One is continued stalemate, leading ultimately to Quebec separation. The other is to embrace the deep diversity formula of belonging to Canada through one's membership in a community whose way of being part of the country might differ from that of another community or communities. Here is how Taylor puts it:

> Suppose that we lived in a country where the common understanding was that there was more than one formula for citizenship and where we could live with the fact that different people related to different formulae. Suppose that we wanted to preserve our common political values, our mode of liberal democracy, and our ways of providing for our common needs – which in fields such as medical care are so different from those of our immediate neighbours. Supposing that we saw that we could best preserve these together, we might even allow ourselves to see that what is specific to each component – yes, even the French language in Quebec – can more effectively be defended within a broader Canadian frame. And we might come to be not dismayed and threatened, but even stimulated and enlarged by the differences we would have to bridge to keep this larger frame. (1992, 199)

The vision Taylor sketches here raises two questions. First, is it achievable? Second, is it desirable? On the first question we can do little more than speculate. The recent history of ethnically-based nationalism suggests that there is more reason to be pessimistic than not. Taylor himself recognizes the somewhat utopian qualities of the deep diversity formula. He believes, however, that the choice is between innovating so as to accommodate the different aspirations of Québécois nationalists, Aboriginal peoples, and other Canadians, or heading toward the same result along a bumpier path and in a spirit of mutual hostility.

But good intentions are unlikely to be enough. In order to operationalize this rather vague formula of deep diversity, it seems inevitable that the supra-community government be weak enough that it poses no potential threat to the identities of the constituent communities. Students of federalism will recognize the likelihood that the governments of the communities will aggressively defend what they believe to be their vital interests, which may lead to increasingly weak ties between communities and a supra-community government that has decreasing legitimacy in the eyes of many citizens. When Taylor muses that members of different communities might recognize that some of those things that they value in common might best be preserved through cooperation within a broader framework, he perhaps fails to reckon with some of the less salubrious realities of politics. Constitutions fit for angels cannot govern human beings.

These questions about the practicality of the deep diversity formula are, admittedly, in the realm of speculation, as is the formula itself, given that it does not operate anywhere in the world. Perhaps it is fairer to address the second question: is the deep diversity formula desirable? More specifically, is it morally superior to what Taylor calls the uniform model of citizenship and political community?

Obviously he thinks so, and in making his case Taylor contrasts the communitarian liberalism that he associates with the deep diversity model to what he calls the atomistic and procedural liberalism best embodied in the politics and society of the United States. Procedural liberalism, he argues, is incapable of achieving a politics of equal respect. Its insistence on the primordial importance of individual rights and that all persons be treated by the state in identical ways blinds it to what Taylor believes are the legitimate claims of community, claims that are essential in order that individuals achieve freedom, authenticity, and dignity. Community is, in other words, essential to achievement of a good life. For this to be realized, some shared conception of the public good is needed. Society and politics must be seen as theatres for the pursuit of common purposes.

This is not the outlook of procedural liberalism. It is suspicious of collective goals and downright hostile toward the notion that the law should be flexible from one group context to another. But in insisting on identical rights, uniformly administered, the procedural liberalism model risks sliding into intolerance and denying equal respect to some groups. Taylor argues that the procedural liberalism so popular in the United States and among English-speaking Canadians is "inhospitable to difference because it can't accommodate what the members of distinct societies really aspire to, which is survival" (1992, 61).

Communitarian liberalism, such as one finds in Quebec, is willing to "weigh the importance of certain forms of uniform treatment against the importance of cultural survival, and opt sometimes in favor of the latter" (1992, 61). This model, Taylor adds, is "grounded very much on judgements about what makes a good life – judgements in which the integrity of cultures has an important place" (1992, 61).

At this point non-communitarians will certainly protest, on a few grounds. First, they will object to the label "liberal" being applied to a model that gives priority to the protection and promotion of collective goals over individual rights and freedoms. Second, they may object to the imputation that official recognition of cultural differences, through the non-uniform application of the law or some variant of Taylor's deep diversity formula, is necessary in order to ensure cultural survival and the individual dignity of a community's members. Third, dissenters may question Taylor's confident claim that one can distinguish fundamental rights, which would apply equally to all individuals, and which should not be infringed in order to protect or promote collective goals, from less fundamental matters where variations in rules and application of the law would be acceptable.

On this last point, Taylor cites the well-known case of signage restrictions in Quebec's Bill 101, arguing that while free speech is fundamental and should not be limited in pursuit of collective goals, the language of commerce does not fall into this category. Some might argue that this distinction diminishes the importance of economic life in human activity and its relationship to personal dignity. But even if one accepts the validity of Taylor's distinction, one might argue that his example does not prove that such distinctions are easy to make or even possible. What about Quebec's legal restrictions on the educational choices available to children whose parents were not educated in English in Canada? Presumably Taylor would argue that no fundamental right is being interfered with here, and that the limitation on individual choice is one that is easily justified in order to protect the French language and culture in Quebec, and thus to maintain the politics of equal respect. Not everyone agrees. Pierre Trudeau, we shall see, views this particular case quite differently.

Taylor's defense of the politics of recognition and deep diversity forms part of the broader argument that he makes about the dilemma of modern people. It is an argument that he has developed in several places, going back to *The Pattern of Politics*, but perhaps most lucidly in his paper entitled "Legitimation Crisis?" There Taylor argued that popular and academic notions of a legitimation crisis in advanced capitalist democracies miss the crucial point. The real crisis of legitimation arises, he argues, not from the contradictions of capitalism or some breakdown of democratic politics, but from the contradiction between two versions of the modern identity.

One stresses human autonomy. Ontologically, it is expressed in Descartes' well known formula, "I think, therefore I am." Taylor puts it this way:

> [T]he modern subject demands autonomy. He is not part of a larger order, but must discern his own purposes ... Thus relative to any social ordering, or supposed "natural" ordering of society, he is seen as originally free. The ordering can only be legitimate if it issues from his consent. (1995, 264)

Against this sort of philosophical background, a life characterized by endless accumulation, retreat into the circle of one's immediate family, and a purely instrumental stance toward nature can all be justified as ways – perhaps the most effective ways – of affirming our autonomy.

The other dominant version of the modern identity has its roots in Rousseau's insistence on the quality of motivation. An individual's choices must accord with his or her true sentiments, the voice of nature as this is expressed through one's reason. This second version of the modern identity, reflected in the Romantic tradition, rejects an instrumental approach to nature in favour of a sympathetic one.

Taylor notes that the first version of the modern identity – we will call it Utilitarian Identity – provides a moral justification for the acquisitive, materialistic, atomistic society. The second version – let us call it Romantic Identity – provides the basis for a critique of the sort of society and life defended by Utilitarian Identity. Both versions, Taylor observes, are part of the modern identity.

The contradictions between them generate both a moral and a political crisis. Taylor writes:

> The ways and forms of [our] accumulative life have to go on appearing as affirmations of freedom and efficacy. Should they be seen as degenerating into mere self-indulgence, then the society undergoes a crisis of confidence. It is a moral crisis, but which is inescapably also a political one; because what is impugned is the definition of the good actually embedded in our practices. Should we come to repudiate this, our allegiance to these practices is threatened, and therefore our society itself. (1995, 277)

A sense of powerlessness and alienation – in the workplace, in politics, in our communities – casts doubt on the legitimacy of a system and way of life whose moral justification is that it enables us to fulfill our autonomous goals. This critique is, of course, quite similar to what Marx, who was also very much influenced by the Romantic tradition, said in his early writings about the alienation of the individual from self, others, and nature. The failure of such a life to nurture public meanings that connect the individual to a wider whole, and the loss of a sympathetic bond with nature that results from the instrumental stance toward the natural world, together produce a sense of malaise. This, Taylor maintains, is the real crisis of legitimacy. It is essentially an identity crisis produced by the contradictions between Utilitarian Identity and Romantic Identity, contradictions sharpened by the hyperthophies of mass-consumption atomistic societies.

These hypertrophies take three forms. First, the ability to produce an unending stream of consumer goods whose relationship to human needs and happiness becomes increasingly dubious ends by discrediting the consumer standard of individual happiness and societal welfare. Second, the culture of self-fulfillment contributes to the fragmentation of the family and thus helps generate the most extreme form of social atomism. Third, increasing levels of urbanization and mobility generate an expansion of the public sector, but the costs and bureaucratization that accompany this growth result in a popular backlash (1985e, 282–6). Taylor sums up the dilemma this way:

> [W]e live in a society whose practices embody a certain notion of identity, and the human good. This must be ours, or we cannot give this society

our allegiance; we are alienated from it ... If these practices which supposedly embody the modern identity can be shown to lead in fact to some such failure to achieve it ... then our allegiance to them is shaken; and perhaps our faith in the conception of the modern identity is shaken as well. We turn to other models. (1985e, 287)

The model that Taylor proposes is liberal communitarianism, a model organized around the modern individual's desire to achieve a personal authenticity and sense of dignity that connect him or her to something beyond the boundaries of self. As Taylor acknowledges in *Sources of the Self*, his is an enterprise of retrieval; an attempt to recover what is best in the modern identity through reasserting the individual's need for public meanings and collective purposes. In this way, he believes, can the malaise of modernity be overcome.

CONCLUSION

In a body of writing as voluminous and wide-ranging as Taylor's it might seem misguided and even futile to search for a dominant theme that informs his approach to politics. But in *Sources of the Self* Taylor identifies this theme. He writes that his purpose is what he calls "retrieval;" the rediscovery of Romantic notions of human freedom and personal identity that are in harmony with and rooted in a sense of community. Rereading his earlier work it becomes clear that this always has been Taylor's goal as a philosopher engaged in the world. Woven through the pattern of his writings on Canadian politics, nationalism, multiculturalism, and the human condition in capitalist democracies is Taylor's belief that the issues of equality and freedom cannot be dealt with meaningfully apart from the question of community. In some ways community is the primordial value for Taylor, in that it is the necessary condition for the dignity of individuals, for personal freedom that is not alienating and socially destructive, and for a moral order that enables people to live good and virtuous lives.

Taylor's impact on the Canadian political scene has been chiefly indirect, but has been no less significant for that. His quixotic forays into party politics and the other ways in which he has been directly engaged in public life, as a commentator on contemporary issues and as a participant in the work of the Commission on the

Political and Constitutional Future of Quebec (1990–91), pale alongside the impact that his writings have had on the contours of political debate on the Canadian left and among members of the intellectual class. During the 1960s and 1970s Taylor was one of Canada's leading intellectual voices on such issues as corporate power, foreign ownership, American cultural domination, and the causes and remedies for social injustice in Canada. Over the last two decades his issue focus has shifted somewhat to multiculturalism, constitutional solutions to French-English conflict, and identity politics. His work was and still is in the must-read category for Canada's political intelligentsia who, in turn, distill, propagate, and react to the arguments and ideas that he has done so much to sow.

CHAPTER SEVEN

The Universalist Liberalism of Pierre Trudeau

Pierre Trudeau, more than any other person, influenced the course of Canadian history in the twentieth century. From his entry into federal politics in 1965 to his resignation as leader of the Liberal Party and prime minister of Canada in 1984, Trudeau was at the centre of Canadian political life. Even before joining the Liberals in Ottawa Trudeau was an important intellectual figure in Canada and in the politics of his home province, Quebec. And after his departure from public life he continued to shape Canadian politics through his influential condemnations of the Meech Lake and Charlottetown Accords on constitutional reform.

Writing about the political ideas of someone who has been both "philosopher" and "king" presents a singular dilemma. Should he be judged by his words or by his deeds?, for it is notoriously true that the exercise of power typically requires that one's ideals be compromised and perhaps even abandoned. This is particularly true when these ideals are ones that are radically at odds with what might be called establishment values and institutions. Should, for example, a judgment of Mackenzie King's political ideas rest chiefly on a reading of *Industry and Humanity*, his paeon to liberal corporatism, or on King's twenty-two year record as a prime minister who showed little inclination to push the grand vision sketched so lovingly in what King himself thought of as the main distillation of his philosophy?

There are those who insist that Pierre Trudeau revealed his authentic self after entering federal politics, and that this self was not what his earlier writings and activities led one to expect. Indeed it quickly became stylish for those on the political left – Trudeau's erstwhile colleagues and soul-mates – to accuse him of being just another bourgeois politician. Charles Taylor, who ran against Trudeau in the 1965 and 1968 federal elections, sketched an unflattering portrait of Trudeau the NYL (New Young Leader), a telegenic embodiment of what Taylor and the left dismissed as the politics of (phoney) consensus. Even his liberalism was called into doubt by many when, during the 1970 October Crisis, Trudeau decided to invoke the War Measures Act. The decision to introduce wage and price controls in 1974 was, for most left-leaning intellectuals, the final proof of his betrayal of the social democratic principles and rights (in this case collective bargaining rights) he had so staunchly defended in an earlier life. But perhaps the loudest and most persistent charge of *volte-face* was that Trudeau, once an unflinching advocate of provincial rights and critic of Ottawa's intrusions onto the constitutional turf of the provinces, became as prime minister the centralizer *par excellence*. On this, if nothing else, Quebec separatists and alienated westerners were able to agree.

In fact, however, Trudeau in power always remained faithful to the core of the political philosophy that he developed and expounded before joining the Liberal Party. It is a philosophy that is liberal, respectful of both individual and group rights, grounded on the Enlightenment's faith in reason, suspicious of communitarian claims, and unflinchingly opposed to nationalism. No single label does justice to the complex and coherent body of ideas that comprise Trudeau's political philosophy. Nonetheless, just as a concern with community gives Taylor's thought its distinctive cast, the character of Trudeau's thought is strongly influenced by the primary importance he assigns to individual freedom.

Trudeau is not, however, a primacy-of-individual rights liberal after the fashion of a Robert Nozick. His liberalism has other roots and leads in directions that certainly are not those of an American-style libertarian. Indeed, we argue that Trudeau's liberal philosophy, like that of Frank Underhill, Eugene Forsey, and F.R. Scott, is solidly in the Canadian tradition of individualism tempered by a commitment to social justice. In Trudeau's case this commitment seems to have its inspiration in Catholic social doctrine more than in the secular and materialist philosophies that influenced so many of his erstwhile colleagues on the Canadian left. He mentions Nicolai Berdyayev, Emmanuel Mounier, and Jacques Maritain as major influences on his philosophical development. Despite the charges of left-wing sympathies that critics regularly hurled at Trudeau, it is clear that his reformist impulses owed more to Maritain than Marx.

This point about influences on Trudeau's thought deserves a moment's reflection. Perhaps because of the very public nature of his career, but also because his writings lack the sort of depth that one finds in the work of a professional philosopher like Taylor, Trudeau's thought has often been "explained" in terms of the social and psychological influences argued to have shaped his personality and philosophy. Although biography is interesting and valuable in its own right, this approach does not do justice to the ideas of the person who, perhaps more than anyone else, has defined what it means to be a liberal in Canadian politics.

FREEDOM

Given Trudeau's well-known antipathy toward ethnic nationalism and his longstanding advocacy of better protection for individual rights in Canada, it is not surprising that his thought has usually been characterized as individualist. The individual's freedom to choose is a prominent theme running throughout his writings and political career. It forms the basis for his attacks on the traditional nationalism of French-speaking Quebec in *La Grève de l'amiante* and in the pages of *Cité libre*. It surfaces in the reforms to Canada's divorce law introduced when Trudeau was Minister of Justice, in his elimination of homosexuality as an offence under the criminal code ("The state has no business in the bedrooms of the nation."), and in the Charter of Rights and Freedoms passed during the life of his last government. But Trudeau's strong commitment to individual freedom has roots that are poorly understood.

In *Towards a Just Society*, written several years after his resignation as leader of the Liberal Party, Trudeau states, "I have long believed that freedom is the most important value of a just society, and the exercise of freedom its principal characteristic" (357). His writings and political career demonstrate the truth of this claim.

Individual freedom is anterior to all other values in his political philosophy, and provides the benchmark for his assessment of social arrangements, cultures, and governments.

The roots of his preoccupation with freedom reach back to Quebec of the 1930s and 1940s, a period marked by official disdain for civil liberties and a dominant ideology that was hostile to liberal notions of freedom and democratic politics. The years of what has been called *la grande noirceur* were analyzed by Trudeau in his contributions to *La Grève de l'amiante*. What emerged from his root-and-branch critique of thought and practice in Quebec at mid-century was Trudeau's anti-nationalism, his sympathy for interventionist economics, and a politics that combined elements of socialism and liberalism. It was a critique and a philosophy very much in tune with the thinking of the Canadian intellectual left, as represented by such figures as F.R. Scott, Frank Underhill, and Eugene Forsey.

Trudeau himself writes that his participation in the Asbestos Strike was motivated by a concern to promote equality in a society whose ruling elites were notoriously unsympathetic to working-class interests and whose conception of equality had everything to do with the rights and preservation of *la race* and nothing to do with socio-economic inequalities. But, he adds, the equality he fought for was not, in his words, "the procrustean kind of equality where everyone is raised or lowered to a kind of middle ground" (Trudeau and Axworthy 1990, 358). It was equality of opportunity or, one might say, an equal opportunity to experience freedom. Equality's justification is the realization of individual freedom. And what does Trudeau believe to be freedom's justification?

At the core of his commitment to freedom is a particular conception of human dignity, as well as a Kantian notion of virtue. Unlike Taylor, Trudeau does not dwell on these matters directly and at length. Instead, one is required to draw inferences about his philosophy from his political writings. Perhaps the major exception to the rule is the series of articles that appeared in *Vrai* in 1958, and which was published several years later in English under the title *Approaches to Politics*. Here one gets a fairly unfiltered sense of the larger premises underpinning Trudeau's politics.

For Trudeau, it is the ability to make enlightened choices that gives human beings dignity. The constraints placed upon human freedom by society are justified only because and to the extent that they assist men and women in leading lives that make such choices possible. But it is not the experience of being free to choose that gives the act dignity. It is the enlightened character of the choice. "[T]he only good action" Trudeau writes, "of real moral value, is a voluntary action, chosen by the enlightened thinking of the person who performs it" (1970b, 36).

There are obvious echoes of Kant here. They become unmistakable when Trudeau discusses the purpose of laws. It is, he says, "to educate the citizen in the common good, and persuade him to behave in the public interest, rather than to command and constrain" (1970b, 50). Following Kant, Trudeau links these concepts of the "common good" and the "public interest" to individual freedom and virtue. To be free and virtuous is impossible outside of society, in other words, apart from some notion of the collective good. Freedom is not its own justification.

What is freedom's justification, according to Trudeau? At this point it is necessary to say something about the spiritual sources of Trudeau's political philosophy, in particular those Christian thinkers to whom he attributes a significant influence on the formation of his own ideas. Among the most important of these thinkers are Nikolai Berdyayev and Emmanuel Mounier. In an interview that Trudeau gave in 1970, he declared that Berdyayev's writings had been particularly important in shaping his own philosophy.

Berdyayev is a founder of Christian existentialism, whose ideas influenced the development of the personalist philosophy expressed by Mounier and others of his generation. Personality, says Berdyayev, is the individual spirit that links a person to God and, therefore, to the universal. It is a sort of crossroads where individual experience intersects the spiritual quality that all people share, and which forms the basis for the equal dignity of all human beings.

Berdyayev's Christian existentialism influenced the generation of personalists to whom Trudeau attributes significant influence on his own intellectual development. The personalist approach, as articulated by Mounier and in the pages of *L'Esprit*, locates the sources of human dignity and the meaningfulness of one's life in the individual's own experiences. It is implacably opposed to those theories which maintain that the individual's dignity depends on his or her identification with communities, however these may be defined. On this point Trudeau quotes Ernest Renan and J.T. Delos. Renan argues that "Man is bound neither to his language nor to his race;

he is bound only to himself because he is a free agent, or in other words a moral being" (quoted in *Federalism and the French Canadians*, 1968, 159). Delos echoes this view when he asks "whether it is not a denial of Man's dignity to reduce him to mere identification with any particular mass of humanity" (1967, 159).

This question of human dignity – what are its sources, and what ideas and social arrangements promote it and which ones threaten it – is crucial to understanding the different ways in which Trudeau and Taylor conceive of freedom. Taylor argues that the individual's experience of dignity is inseparable from the relationship to the community/ies that give each life meaning. For Taylor, dignity is generated dialogically and is based on a person's identification with a communal group that makes sense of and affirms the meaning of his or her own life. Freedom too, according to Taylor, can only be experienced through communal associations. A freely willed act is one taken in awareness of moral horizons linking the individual to the community.

This is where a parting of the ways occurs. Trudeau is much more comfortable with the idea of *man-in-society*, as opposed to the communitarian conceptual framework that Taylor favours. Whereas Taylor sees such communal associations as the nation as being potentially freedom-enriching and vital to human dignity, Trudeau has doubts on both counts. To understand why, it is useful to refer to Jacques Maritain's observations on the distinction between communities and societies, observations with which Trudeau would certainly agree.[1]

Community, Maritain observes, is a phenomenon that arises naturally and inevitably in human relations, where "the collective patterns of feeling ... have the upper hand over personal consciousness, and man appears as a product of the social group" (1952, 4). Society, by contrast, is the fruit of human reason and personal freedom. "In society," he writes, "personal consciousness retains priority, the social group is shaped by men, and social relations proceed from ... the voluntary determination of human persons" (1952, 4).

Society involves, Maritain argues, a higher form of human relationships than community. This is because society is based on reason, consent, and law. "In society, social pressure derives from law or rational regulations, or from an idea of the common aim; it calls forth personal conscience and liberty, which must obey the law freely" (1952, 4). Communities, by contrast, are more or less deterministic human relationships that are rooted in nature. Maritain acknowledges that communal associations are normal and good, but he insists on the moral superiority of society. This is because the individual's actions, commitments and purposes are, ideally at any rate, based on personal conscience and free will. Although Maritain does not say it, one suspects that he would agree that the human person can find in community such important conditions as solidarity and personal esteem, but only in society can the individual experience dignity, because only in society (not community) is he or she truly a free agent. What Maritain does say is this:

> [Community] does not appeal to the freedom and responsibility of personal conscience, it instils in human persons a second nature. It is a general pattern in private life, it does not know any principle of public order. (1952, 6)

Communities will always exist within political society, but political society should never be based on the ties of community. This, Maritain argues, is the mistake of modern nationalism, which must always end by denying individual freedom and diminishing human dignity.

Trudeau certainly agrees. He shares Maritain's disdain for the idea of the nation-state, viewing it as the enemy of personal freedom, about which more will be said later in this chapter. The contrast between Trudeau and Taylor should not, however, be pushed too hard. Taylor certainly recognizes the totalitarian dangers that nationalism has often created. Nevertheless, he is far more sanguine than Trudeau about the ability of a political society organized according to the national principle – an independent Quebec, for example – to respect fundamental freedoms. He is even more convinced that communal associations based on ethnicity, language, and other attributes are vital to human dignity in an age that leaves people increasingly isolated from one another and, moreover, that these communal identities need to be recognized by political society. Trudeau, however, doubts that this recognition actually promotes human dignity.

The difference between Trudeau's and Taylor's conception of freedom hinges on dignity. Both have a positive notion of freedom as being linked to personal fulfillment and the achievement of a good life. Neither has any time for the negative conception of freedom as the absence of constraint that is favoured by some shades of libertarianism. Freedom is not, they would agree, its own justification. Trudeau would not object to Taylor's insistence that genuine freedom requires that it be exercised against moral horizons. The notion of moral horizons links freedom to human dignity; it invests freedom with a moral dimension. But what are these "moral horizons"? This is where agreement breaks down.

Taylor's moral horizons are based on his dialogical view of how human dignity and identity are generated and nurtured. Trudeau's personalist philosophy leads him to view these moral horizons in a rather different way. His notion of dignity depends less on the individual's relationship to groups and more on "dialogue" with the self. When Taylor talks of moral horizons the community inevitably appears. Trudeau's human subject gazing out onto a moral horizon is more of an individualist. Consequently, his perspective on human dignity and freedom is less influenced by collectivist goals.

It is wrong, however, to characterize Trudeau's liberalism as individualistic, as sometimes is done. Here commentators have too often confused Trudeau's personal style with his political philosophy. Both his writings and his career in politics show that Trudeau is comfortable with state planning, skeptical of capitalism, and committed to a redistributive ethos that no liberal of the John Locke/Adam Smith school could ever tolerate. But he can never be entirely at ease with a socialist politics, or any variation of communitarianism, because of his refusal to locate the sources of personal fulfillment and moral goodness in collectivities and their purposes.

In at least one respect, however, Trudeau's liberalism does deserve to be called individualistic. This involves the virtues of competition and the proper role of government in protecting the weak from the strong. It is clear that Trudeau distinguishes between economic forms of competition and those that involve culture. When it comes to economics Trudeau does not hesitate to reject the doctrine of laissez-faire, on the grounds that the unregulated market inevitably destroys the freedom of the weak. Freedom is, in Trudeau's view, inseparable from social justice in a democratic society. The monopolistic tendencies of capital and its indifference to the fate of those who, for whatever reason, cannot compete in the marketplace, undermine the possibility of real freedom for most people. When it comes to economics, Trudeau's liberalism is of the traditionally Canadian sort: regulation of business and the provision of public services are considered essential responsibilities of the state.

But on the matter of culture, Trudeau is more ambivalent about the state's role. He recognizes that the tendency of modern capitalism and technology is to erode cultural differences between societies. "Technology," he writes, "... tends to minimize the values that let a human being acquire and retain his own identity, values that I am grouping here under the vague term 'cultural.' The political order created by the state must struggle against this kind of depersonalization by pursuing cultural objectives" (1968, 28–9). Public broadcasting, multicultural programs, state support for the arts: the Trudeau years saw the continuation and, in some cases, the expansion of these sorts of policies to protect and promote cultural values. At what point, however, does the case for policies that preserve cultural identity/ies recede before the threat such measures may pose to freedom of choice?

Trudeau's answer is ambiguous. At the same time as he defends safeguards for indigenous cultural values he is highly critical of certain forms of cultural protectionism. Trudeau is especially critical of any sort of ethnic or linguistic protectionism for French in Quebec. "[A] culture makes progress," he argues "through the exchange of ideas and through challenge" (1968, 33). Trudeau's insistence on the importance of competition in the realm of ideas and culture, and the withering disdain he often expresses for values that can only survive with the assistance of a state life-support system, are recurring themes in his writings. It is not entirely clear, however, why restrictions on, say, American magazines or television programs are acceptable in order to protect Canadian identity, while limits on the use of English to protect the "French-ness" of Quebec are not. Even if one grants that prohibiting a non-anglophone parent from sending his or her child to a publicly-funded English school is a more serious matter than requiring broadcasters to carry a certain amount of Canadian programming (while still allowing them to show lots of the popular American stuff), this leaves unanswered the question of when cultural competition is harmful and when it is desirable.

Trudeau's answer, presumably, would be that Quebec's language protectionism is based on "a definition of the common good as a function of an ethnic group, rather than of all the people, regardless of characteristics" (1968, 169). In other words, it effectively denies important aspects of social pluralism in Quebec and elevates the preservation and promotion of the French-speaking community to a level that threatens individual freedom and dignity. Canadian content regulations, on the other hand, are not associated with the status of any particular ethnic group, nor do they exclude competing cultural values. They are intended to maintain and promote Canadian identity, but they attempt to do so by ensuring the availability of Canadian programming rather than by banning the competition. There is, in fact, no contradiction between Trudeau's defense of Canadian nationalism in the face of Americanizing influences and his rejection of Quebec nationalists' efforts to protect the French language from anglicizing pressures.

In the end, it seems pretty clear that Trudeau is committed to competition in the realm of culture and ideas and that like Henri Bourassa, another believer in the possibility of a bilingual Canada, Trudeau has faith in the ability of the French language and culture to compete with English so long as their constitutional equality is respected in public life. In "The New Treason of the Intellectuals" he writes,

> The day of language barriers is finished, at least as far as science and culture are concerned; and if Quebec's intellectuals refuse to master another language than their own, if they will recognize no loyalty but to their nation, then they may be renouncing forever their place among the world's intellectual elite. (1968, 174)

Trudeau rejects the collectivist (and, he would say, reactionary) idea that values, traditions, and languages deserve respect and protection as a matter of right and justice. Too much cultural protectionism, he argues, inevitably shades into intolerance and finally a totalitarian denial of personal freedom in the name of group dignity.

A theory of freedom is also a theory of authority: when and in what forms community-imposed limits on personal freedom are justified. Trudeau's thoughts on authority were first set forth systematically in the series of articles that he wrote for *Vrai* in 1958. In the fourth of these articles he provides a classic liberal formulation of authority's raison d'être:

> The purpose of living in society is that every man may fulfil himself as far as possible. Authority has no justification except to allow the establishment and development of a system that encourages such fulfillment. (1970b, 34)

Rights, Trudeau argues, should be treated as being "anterior to the very existence of the state" (1970b, 8). Whatever authority over the individual is permitted the state should be delegated "grudgingly" (1970b, 50) and only so as to ensure order and social justice. In words that echo Kant, Trudeau writes, "The real purpose of laws, then, is to educate the citizen in the common good, and persuade him to behave in the public interest, rather than to command and constrain" (1970b, 50).

Trudeau's views on authority are particularly important in light of his government's 1970 invocation of the War Measures Act. Many of his critics charge that recourse to this Act – the first and only time it has been used in peacetime – demonstrated an authoritarianism which belied his fine words about freedom and the importance of rights. The Act allowed the federal government to suspend normal civil liberties in order to deal with a war or "apprehended insurrection."[2] Trudeau's critics argue that invocation of the Act was an excessive response to the political terrorism perpetrated by the Front de libération du Québec (FLQ) and, moreover, that it was used as an opportunity to arrest and harass people whose separatist views Trudeau despised.

It is easy to second-guess Trudeau's response to the kidnapping of James Cross and Pierre Laporte, and the killing of the latter. And it certainly is not our intention to revisit one of the most discussed controveries in Canada's recent history. From the standpoint of what it reveals about Trudeau's political philosophy, however, the decision to invoke the War Measures Act is noteworthy. Two decades earlier, in the series Trudeau wrote for *Vrai*, he said this about the legitimate use of coercion by the state:

> [T]he state must use force only to the extent that individuals or organizations try to use it themselves against the common good. If it is true that in the last analysis the state must retain the monopoly of force, the purpose is less to use it than to prevent someone else from usurping the thunderbolts. (1970b, 77)

This is precisely the argument Trudeau made in justifying the suspension of civil liberties during the FLQ crisis. The question will always remain, did the events of October 1970 constitute a serious threat to the authority of the Quebec government and to the stability of public order on which peaceful democratic politics and respect for personal freedoms depends? On this point it is worth remembering that as respected and tempermentally cautious a person as Claude Ryan, at the time editor of *Le Devoir*, was talking seriously about the possibility of a provisional government to replace that of Quebec's Liberal premier Robert Bourassa. Those who prefer to attribute underhanded and illiberal motives to Pierre Trudeau will surely do so. There were, however, some grounds for believing that there existed a danger of "someone else ... usurping the thunderbolts" that properly belonged to a democratically elected government.

Those who sympathized with the FLQ, if not with its resort to murder, would argue that the centuries-old subjugation of francophones by anglophones and the denial of Québécois' right to self-determination constituted a more serious form of violence than a few bombings. Using liberal democratic arguments similar to those of John Locke and the American revolutionaries who took Locke as their bible, they maintained that civil disobedience and the use of force are justified when state rule is no longer based on the consent of the people. This is a principle with which Trudeau agrees. In an interview he gave in 1970, Trudeau said,

> If those who govern the society in which you live and who direct its future do not respect the freedom of expression, of religion, of choice, and assembly, and if there exists no democratic method of changing this order of things in a peaceful, reasonable way, and if, consequently, certains ideas in which you believe are banned, there is only one means for you to defend yourself against the violence inflicted on you: it is to use violence in turn. (1972, 128, our translation)

But while Trudeau agrees in principle that citizens may be justified, in the circumstances he describes, in using violence against the state, he rejects the notion that these circumstances have existed in Canada.

Personal freedom is central to Trudeau's political philosophy. But his conception of freedom is developed within a broader context of what a just society should look like. "For where is the justice," he asks, "in a country in which an individual has the freedom to be totally fulfilled, but where inequality denies him the means?" (1990, 358) We turn now to his thoughts on equality.

EQUALITY

It is rare for Canadian politicians to quote poets and nineteenth-century French novelists, and rarer still that they quote them extemporaneously. Pierre Trudeau had this unusual penchant. Two of the literary figures whose work he favoured were W.H. Auden and Anatole France. In conversation with CBC broadcaster Peter Gzowski several years after resigning as prime minister, Trudeau repeated Auden's observation that the law exists to protect the poor and disadvantaged, the rich and powerful having no special need of it to protect their interests. On the same theme Trudeau would occasionally quote Anatole France's well-known observation that the law in its majesty prohibits both the rich and the poor from sleeping under the bridges of Paris.

Some of Trudeau's critics, including Charles Taylor, would dismiss these sentiments as not truly reflecting the politics of the Pierre Trudeau who led Canada for fifteen years. Left-wing academics and social critics seldom had a kind word for Trudeau, whom they saw as the prime minister who twice introduced wage controls (wage controls across the economy in 1975–78, and for federal public servants in 1981–82), and whom they regularly pilloried as just another bourgeois politician.[3] The socialist principles and sympathies that Trudeau expressed before his entry into the Liberal Party were, they argued, jettisoned once he became part of this country's political Establishment.

To repeat what we said earlier, our intention is not to attempt judgment on Trudeau's years in federal politics, except insofar as this helps to understand his philosophy of politics. It would be unfair, however, to look only at the policies of the Trudeau years. Would anyone think of trying to understand the thought of Václav Havel based only on his years as premier of the Czech Republic, or the political philosophy of Mario Vargas Llosa by looking only at his political record as president of Venezuela? Trudeau has written extensively on the subject of equality, and these writings – not the compromises dictated by politics – provide an important guide to his thought.

Trudeau's baptism in politics took place in class struggle. The strike against the Johns-Manville asbestos mines at Thetford and Asbestos, Quebec was the first major demonstration of worker solidarity against the power of multinational capital and the political and religious elites whose sympathies were clearly with the owners. Trudeau's role in the events that unfolded at Thetford and Asbestos was actually quite peripheral. His chief contribution was as editor and contributor to a volume of essays entitled *La Grève de l'amiante*, in which various aspects of the background to the strike and the conflict itself were analyzed by Quebec economists, sociologists, journalists, lawyers, and trade unionists.

In his two contributions to this book, Trudeau shows himself to be quite familiar with marxian theories of political economy. He does not hesitate to use terms like "proletariat," "bourgeoisie," and "property-owning class." Trudeau offers an ardent defense of the proletariat and unions as the only hope for achieving democracy and social justice. In his epilogue to the volume he rejects the charge that he and his "comrades" (his word) have fallen victim to what Raymond Aron called "the opium of the intellectuals" (494). Nevertheless, there is a rather naively romantic tone evident in some of Trudeau's observations about the "people," the "masses," and the "working class" (see 392–3).

Trudeau the critic of capitalism, whose ideas about economics and the state appear to have been strongly influenced by the experiences of the Depression and World War II, places his faith in "a certain amount of state planning" and "nationalization of the principle means of production" (403). However, he is never as critical of capitalism in either moral or efficiency terms as Taylor is. Trudeau's obvious reservations about economic laissez-faire are permeated by a streak of economic liberalism that arises from his awareness of how internationalizing tendencies in world trade render national boundaries and forms of protectionism increasingly obsolete (see 1968, 13). Nevertheless, a fundamental skepticism about markets and businesspeople, and a belief in the efficacy of the public sector and planning, stayed with Trudeau throughout all phases of his political career.

In his introduction to *La Grève de l'amiante*, Trudeau expresses his impatience with what he calls the ethnocentrism of Quebec intellectuals. "The common good," he writes, "would probably have been better served if our researchers were less upset by the unequal distribution of provincial wealth from the ethnic point of view, and more by the unequal distribution inherent in liberal economics from the viewpoint of social classes" (1970a, 45). This is a theme that Trudeau would amplify in subsequent writings. Although far from indifferent to ethnically-based inequalities, he always considered class-based differences to be a more serious matter. Equality of economic opportunity is, according to Trudeau, more vital to human dignity and the realization of personal freedom than is one's ethnic identity. Consequently, and unlike many Quebec intellectuals of his generation, when Trudeau is critical of English Canadians' discrimination against their French compatriots, the injustice he inveighs against has little to do with national pride but much to do with the economic effects of ethnic inequalities.

What emerges from Trudeau's comprehensive critique of thought and practice in Quebec on the eve of the Asbestos Strike is his anti-nationalism, his faith in interventionist economics, and a politics very much in tune with the thinking of the Canadian left of the 1940s, as represented in the writings of those like F.R. Scott and Eugene Forsey. The notion of justice that Trudeau expresses is not rooted in a materialistic philosophy or ontology, despite his frequent use of terms and concepts culled from the marxian vocabulary. Rather, its roots are Christian and spiritual, as was typical of the Canadian left during this era. In attacking the Church authorities who sided with "the rights of management" (1970a, 402) against the striking workers, Trudeau accuses them of having abandoned their spiritual vocation in favour of an authoritarian defense of an unjust status quo. He leaves no doubt that in his view, the class struggle that unfolded at Asbestos and Thetford was fundamentally a spiritual conflict between opposing social philosophies. He asks,

> [A]t Asbestos, where were the partisans of the human spirit to be found? On the side of the bosses who wish to allow the workers to earn his steak, on condition that he not aspire to deal on an equal footing with the monied powers? Or on the side of the unions who naively believed the moment had come to go beyond purely material results and put in place the basis for a society of equals? (1970a, 402)

Equality of economic opportunity, Trudeau maintains, is the basis for a just society. In order to advance toward this goal, the state must play an important role. Individually, men and women have neither the time nor the means to ensure that they are being fairly treated by those more powerful than them. "So if the citizen wants to avoid being ordered about against his will" says Trudeau, "he must provide himself with a protector in the form of a state strong enough to subordinate to the pubic good all the individuals and organisms that go to make up society" (1970b, 85). But not only must the state's authority be broad, the competence and commitment of those who work for the state must be at least equal to those in the private sector. Otherwise, says Trudeau, "it is impossible to ensure the triumph of the public over the private good" (1970b, 85).

A strong state combined with universal suffrage is not, Trudeau recognizes, a guarantee that democratic laws will be passed and justice done. But a weak state and an ideological climate hostile to its authority ensure that government will not be able to perform what Trudeau argues is its fundamental role, the protection of each individual's rights and in particular, those of the weak. Like Charles Taylor, Trudeau has little use for the libertarian, anti-government philosophy that is an important part of the American political tradition. And like Taylor, strands of anti-American sentiment and skepticism about free market economics are woven throughout his thought and influence his ideas about the state's authority.

In a passage that could as well have been written by Taylor, Trudeau writes,

> Technology ... tends to minimize the values that let a human being acquire and retain his own identity, values that I am grouping here under the vague term "cultural." The political order created by the state must struggle against this kind of depersonalization by pursuing cultural objectives. (1968, 28–9)

The state has a responsibility, Trudeau argues, to "intervene to ensure the survival of cultural values in danger of being swamped by a flood of dollars" (1968, 29). In typical Trudeau fashion, however, he immediately adds that there should be limits to this cultural protectionism. He warns against the possible slide into state paternalism and the promotion of hot-house culture. "[I]n the long term," he says, "the state should ideally promote an open culture" (1968, 29).

There is a recurring ambivalence in Trudeau's thought between competition and protection for the weak. His sense of justice and his disdain for the purely materialist values associated with capitalism lead him to defend state intervention in culture and economics. At the same time it is apparent that Trudeau has greatest respect for those values which, faced with competition, win the day. Thus, his support for public investment to promote cultural values that are neglected or even negated by the market stops far short of banning competition. A similar line of reasoning runs through Trudeau's views on nationalistic policies (discussed later in this chapter). His sympathy for the preservation of languages and national traditions collides with his belief that, in the end, competition will decide the language of businesspeople, scientists, and artists, and the values of the general population. Moreover, the measures necessary to overcome the long-term pressure of these competitive forces are, Trudeau would argue, incompatible with respect for personal freedom and undemocratic.

Compared to Taylor's, Trudeau's anti-Americanism is quite mild. This is true of his pre-Liberal Party days and not simply of his years as a federal politician, when prudence would have been expected to cool the ardour with which such sentiments might be expressed. Trudeau in power displayed some sympathy for the policies advocated by left nationalists, including the creation of the Canada Development Corporation (1971), the "Third Option" trade diversification policy (1973), Petro Canada (1974), restrictions on foreign investment through the Foreign Investment Review Agency (1974), and expanding domestic ownership of the petroleum industry through the National Energy Programme (1980). All of these were considered little better than half-measures by the political left, but they did provide evidence of Trudeau's general agreement with the left nationalist view that American domination of the Canadian economy was, on balance, something to be regretted.

The catalogue of left nationalist grievances against Canada's dependence on American capital and trade is long and well known.[4] At a general level, beyond the specific claims made about harm done to the economy, political sovereignty, or the ability to maintain distinctive social programs in Canada, this critique is informed by a dislike of American culture in the broad sense of the word. This dislike regularly surfaces in discussions of the health care, education, and welfare systems of Canada and the United States, and boils down to a simple formula: Canadians are more compassionate and sharing than their American counterparts and they expect their governments to defend policies that reflect this cultural difference. What Trudeau calls the "Just Society" involves state intervention that embodies the collectivist ethos which sets Canadians apart from their southern neighbours.

Trudeau shares this distaste for American cultural values, if not all the specific grievances that left nationalists have against the United States. As prime minister he was clearly more comfortable in the company of a Helmut Schmidt or François Mitterrand than of a Richard Nixon or Ronald Reagan. The social democratic notion of distributive equality appeals to him more than the pioneer equality associated with the notion of "rugged individualism." The collectivist sense of justice that one finds in Trudeau's thought is, however, significantly different from Taylor's communitarian sense of justice. As in the case of freedom, the key to understanding their differences seems to lie in how they conceive of individual dignity.

Dignity is by its very nature a state of mind that depends on others, or at least one's perception of others' thoughts about oneself. Even the hermit cannot be free of the importance of the "other" when it comes to personal dignity. Henry David Thoreau, one of the best known philosophers of solitude, professed to be absolutely indifferent to the views of his neighbours concerning his way of life. Nevertheless, his belief that the life he chose was dignified (Thoreau was not given to using the word "dignified." He would have favoured "poetic" or "truly human.") was derived in what Taylor would call a dialogical manner: through interaction with Thoreau's ideas about human society, the great thinkers whose works he read, God-in-nature, and no doubt those like Ralph Waldo Emerson who were his friends.

The difference between Trudeau and Taylor involves the relative influence they attach to those outside the individual on one's dignity. Trudeau's personalist philosophy leads him to place less emphasis on these others than is the case with Taylor, whose notion of individual dignity is inseparable from communal identity. While recognizing that equality and dignity have collective dimensions, Trudeau is always firm in maintaining that "only the individual is the possessor of rights" (1990, 364) and in rejecting any concept of human dignity, such as that associated with nationalism, that locates the primary sources of dignity in one's association with a collectivity that is more narrowly drawn than society. Dignity and equality are states that can only be achieved in society, he would argue, but they do not require that one's communal identity(ies) be central to personal fulfillment, or what Taylor calls the achievement of authenticity. On the contrary, elevating communal identity to the top rung in politics, and all this may entail such as constitutional recognition of a community's distinct status and rights and guaranteeing these rights to the community as such, rather than to individuals, actually undermines dignity and equality, according to Trudeau.

As prime minister, Trudeau was regularly attacked from the left for not doing enough to promote socio-economic equality. It is probably fair to say that Trudeau in power did not push the cause of social reform as far as he would have preferred, although he does mention a decrease in poverty, entrenchment of Charter rights for the disabled and visible minorities, progress toward various forms of self-government for Aboriginal peoples, and programs targeted at young Canadians as major accomplishments during his tenure as prime minister (1990, 380). Trudeau's commitment to social reform was, however, tempered by what he would doubtless call political realism – a quality which, in the years before he entered federal politics, he often accused his social democratic colleagues of lacking. On both philosophical and tactical grounds Trudeau argued that social reformers should abandon their centralist politics and their view of the provinces as constitutionally subordinate to Ottawa. "Federalism must be welcomed," he argued, "as a valuable tool which permits dynamic parties to plant socialist governments in certain provinces, from which the seed of radicalism can slowly spread" (1968, 127). If this means that social reform becomes a sort of patchwork quilt, advancing at different stages in different provinces, so be it. The central planning model was, Trudeau argued, unachievable on strategic grounds and undesirable in any case because of its disregard for provincial rights and the significant differences between provincial societies.

Trudeau's sense of political realism was often apparent during his years in power. One of the most revealing episodes involved his reaction to the 1983 publication of the Canadian bishops' statement on the economy, *Ethical Reflections on the Economic Crisis*. The ideas expressed by the bishops were not very different from those of the Trudeau who wrote "Quebec on the Eve of the Asbestos Strike." Instead of a sympathetic hearing, however, the bishops' economic analysis was publically denounced by Trudeau as ill-informed meddling in matters outside their competence. The bishops' argument that modern capitalism was fundamentally immoral and their advocacy of what they called the "option for the poor" as the appropriate measure of just government policies were, Trudeau recognized, not terribly useful in any but rhetorical terms. One suspects that Trudeau was not, in principle, completely out of sympathy with the bishops. But theirs was precisely the sort of idealism in politics that Trudeau had begun to warn against as an active member of the political left in the 1950s.

COMMUNITY

In the heated atmosphere that followed the defeat of the Meech Lake Accord, the Quebec government established the Commission sur l'avenir politique et constitutionnel du Québec (popularly known as the Bélanger-Campeau Commission). One of the Commission's first actions was to invite over one hundred Quebec experts on the constitution to express their views on the nature of the problem and how to fix it. Pierre Trudeau, one-time professor of constitutional law, former prime minister of Canada, and arguably the most prominent Quebecer of his generation, was not invited to express his views. Asked why Trudeau was excluded from the list of acknowledged experts, the commissioners' response was, "We already know what he would say" – as if there was much that was not predictable in the testimony and written submissions of many of those whom the Commission included.

The commissioners did, however, have a point. Trudeau's public denouncement of the Meech Lake Accord had been crucial in galvanizing public opinon in English Canada against the reforms it proposed, particularly the constitutional recognition of Quebec as a distinct society (as would again happen when he weighed in against the Charlottetown Accord two years later). His attacks on nationalism and on Quebec nationalism and nationalists were matters of public record, dating back to the 1950s. Trudeau had entered federal politics, everyone knew, in order to fight what he saw as a rising tide of Quebec nationalism in the 1960s. Add to this the enmity felt by much of Quebec's political and cultural elites toward Trudeau, whom they perceived as an anti-nationalism zealot with a talent for insulting those who disagreed with him, and Trudeau's exclusion was not surprising.

But the portrayal of Trudeau as an intractable anti-nationalist is an unfair caricature. As Trudeau has written, "It is not the concept of the *nation* that is retrograde; it is the idea that the nation must necessarily be sovereign" (1968, 151). His political philosophy is able to accommodate the existence of national communities within society and even some forms of constitutional recognition for these communities. He rejects, however, the concept of the nation-state – the argument that nations have a right to self-determination – and any form of government that rests on the primordial importance of the nation or of any other collectivity that is defined in racial, ethnic, or cultural terms.

Trudeau's thoughts on nationalism have deep philosophical roots. The influence of Jacques Maritain is evident in the way Trudeau conceives of the appropriate relationship between the individual, the nation, and the state. Maritain distinguishes between *society* and *community*, considering society to be a higher form of human social organization based on reason and personal will. Communities, including nations, are products of "instinct and heredity in given circumstances and historical frameworks" (1952, 3–4). From families to nations, people are destined to feel that they belong to communities. This is a necessary part of the human condition and is often a good thing. But the human associations found in communities are not based on the free exercise of reason. Those in society are, which is why society represents a superior stage in human social evolution.

The state, says Maritain, is that part of society "which specializes in the interests of the whole" (1952, 12). It should, ideally, derive its dignity in the eyes of citizens from the exercise of justice (1952, 19). The *democratic* state cannot be associated with a particular community, such as a national group, without undermining individual freedom and the possibility of democratic government. The concept of the *nation-state*, the idea that the nation has a sort of primordial right to self-determination, is rejected by Maritain as a tragic confusion of the national community and political society. The latter, says Maritain, represents a superior order of social organization, one associated with reason, universalism, and freedom. By contrast, intolerance and the totalitarian state are the consequences of what Maritain dismisses as the "myth of the National State" (Ibid., 7).

The nation may, however, achieve the higher level of social organization characteristic of political society and the state. For this to happen it must be separated from the sort of tribal associations that give rise to demands for the nation-state. The nation must, in fact, be culturally multi-national. Maritain writes,

> [W]hen a *political society* has been formed, especially when it has a century-old experience strengthening genuine civic friendship, it naturally gives rise, within itself, to a *national community* of a higher degree, either with regard to the self-awareness of such an already existing community, or with regard to the very formation of a New National Community in which the various nationalities have been merged. Thus, to the exact contrary of the so-called principle of nationalities, the Nation here depends on the existence of the body politic, not the body politic on the existence of the Nation. The Nation does not become a state. The State causes the Nation to be. (1952, 8)

Those who are familiar with Trudeau's writings will know that these are precisely the arguments Trudeau makes against the nation-state and for the multinational nation, whose existence depends on a shared sense of civic life – in other words, on the state. In words that clearly echo Maritain, Trudeau insists that "From a philosophical point of view, the aim of political society is not the glorification of a 'national fact' (in its ethnic sense). A state that defined its function essentially in terms of ethnic attributes would inevitably become chauvinistic and intolerant" (1952, 4). Like Maritain, Trudeau distinguishes between nations and Nations. The latter category includes those societies like the United States, Switzerland, and France – and Canada, Trudeau would insist! – where ethnically-based nationalities have not been obliterated but exist within a National Community based on shared civic values.

Throughout his adult life Trudeau was unwilling to concede any quarter to ethnic nationalities and the defenders of the nation-state. They are, he believed, corrosive of human dignity. In this he differs sharply from Taylor, who is inclined to sympathize with such demands on the grounds that nationalist sentiments reflect the search for authenticty and meaning in an age that provides little support for the collective meanings that Taylor believes are so vital to human dignity. Whereas Taylor is able to see something morally redeeming in nationalism, as a sort of spiritual balm that enables individuals to overcome the atomism characteristic of modernity, Trudeau expresses the hope that the appeal of nationalism will diminish, to be replaced by "a much more functional approach to the problems of government" (1968, 196). Trudeau argues that nationalistic sentiments and movements belong to a "transitional period in world history," one that will recede in the face of globalizing forces in economics, culture, science and, ultimately, politics. Taylor views the historical role of nationalism quite differently. He sees contemporary nationalism as being generated, or at least maintained, by the search for personal authenticity and the human need for a sense of community that modern social and economic organization does not fulfil. The resurgence of nationalism and the rise of multiculturalism – in a word, the ascendance of the politics of recognition – reflect the human need for collective meanings in an age where technology and economics conspire to deny opportunities for communitarian experiences.

Trudeau does not deny the importance of collective identities and group recognition in politics. It was, after all, his government that passed the Official Languages Act, introduced Canada's policy of official multiculturalism, and proposed a Charter of Rights and Freedoms that includes guarantees for members of official language minorities and Aboriginal peoples. He is very well aware that an individual's dignity may be undermined by social practices and government policies that deny recognition to the group which is crucial to one's identity and self-image. Speaking of the federal government's historically anglophone and British character, Trudeau writes, "[T]he French-Canadian denizens of a Quebec ghetto, stripped of power by centralization, were expected to recognize themselves in a national image which had hardly any French traits…" (1968, 200).

Nevertheless, Trudeau believes that the tide of history runs against nationalism. In a well-known passage from "Federalism, Nationalism, and Reason" he has the following to say about the future of nationalism:

> But in the advanced societies, where the interplay of social forces can be regulated by law, where the centres of political power can be made responsible to the people, where the economic victories are a function of education and automation, where cultural differentiation is submitted to ruthless competition, and where the road to progress lies in the direction of international integration, nationalism will have to be discarded as a rustic and clumsy tool. (1968, 202)

Nationalism, Trudeau argues, will retain its importance in "backward societies" where it will be kept alive by "irrational and brutal forces" (1968, 202). He associates nationalism with "emotions and dreams," "superstition," "magic," and a reactionary exploitative politics. It is, Trudeau maintains, the antithesis of reason and an impossible basis on which to build an advanced society and a democratic politics.

To be sure, Taylor also has little sympathy for the sort of nationalism that would confer citizenship and full rights only on the members of a particular national community, and which strives toward the ideal of the nation-state. His greater tolerance for nationalist demands, such as those in Quebec, derives from his belief that cultural diversity and respect for the rights of minorities can be maintained within the framework of a state which has certain national characteristics, such as the requirements that children be educated in the language of the majority national community and that business be conducted in that language. Trudeau disagrees. Already in 1964 he was expressing the fear that Quebec would pass from "religious confessionality to compulsory linguistic confessionality," where parents would be required by law to send their children to French-speaking schools (1968, 208–9).

There are two features to such a law – which has operated in Quebec, with certain limitations, since 1977 – that Trudeau finds repugnant. First, he considers such restrictions an insult to francophones because they clearly are based on the belief that without this form of protection the French language will lose ground in Quebec. As we discussed earlier, Trudeau always insists on the importance of competition in the fields of culture, science, and technology. Forms of protection that involve the interdiction of competition are, he believes, a demeaning admission of weakness on the part of those whose dignity such measures are supposed to nurture. Protection that Trudeau would find appropriate for those whose weakness derives from their socio-economic conditions and necessary for human dignity, he rejects as an affront to dignity in the realm of culture.

The second feature of restrictive language laws that Trudeau rejects is what he sees as their collectivist ideology. If, as he argues, the community exists and is morally good insofar as it helps ensure individual freedom, laws that limit that freedom in the name of the community and that interpret individual freedom through the prism of the community's "needs" are reactionary. "For the very purpose of a collective system," Trudeau maintains, "is better to ensure personal freedom. (Or else you are a fascist.)" (1968, 209)

Again, the difference between Taylor and Trudeau is more nuanced than stark. Providing conditions that will enable the individual to be free is, they agree, the community's and the state's raison d'être. But Taylor is more likely than Trudeau to see the experience of real freedom as something that requires the affirmation and, if need be, the protection of collective values. The importance Taylor attaches to collective meanings and identities in establishing what he calls the moral horizons of individual choice leads him to accept what might be called *raison de communauté* as a perfectly valid reason for restricting a person's choice. Trudeau, however, detects in *raison de communauté* an incipient collectivism which he believes to be inconsistent with true freedom.

The concept of community with which Trudeau is comfortable with is one that Donald Smiley once described as *political nationality*.[5] It is based on a shared allegiance to a constitution and the state, and a common citizenship whose personal meaning does not depend on cultural affinities but on a desire to continue living together as a Nation (in Trudeau's non-ethnic sense of the word). It is, Trudeau would say, a concept of community that depends on reason. And in ethnically diverse societies a federal form of government is, Trudeau argues, the most successful method of ensuring that regionally based communities are allowed enough scope for expression of their collective identities without undermining the sense of political nationality that binds together citizens of different cultural communities.

How does this compare to Taylor's argument about different ways of belonging to a country, an argument that is able to accommodate special status for Quebec and self-determination for aboriginal communities? In the community that Taylor envisages, what he calls "deep diversity" would be recognized by constitutional arrangements flexible enough to allow different groups of citizens to have various relationships to the central government. Trudeau has always rejected this sort of formula, whether it was packaged as "special status," "distinct society," "self-determination," Joe Clark's "community of communities," or Taylor's deep diversity. His reason for doing so, and a key difference between Trudeau and Taylor in their thinking about community, involves the universalist character of Trudeau's liberalism.

When it comes to their rights and responsibilities, citizens must, Trudeau argues, relate directly to the state, not through the intermediary of communities with which they may identify. This is why he attaches such importance to the Charter of Rights and Freedoms as the embodiment of his vision of Canadian nationhood, or what Smiley called the Canadian political nationality. In providing universal rights to Canadian citizens and in defining rights as belonging to individuals rather than collectivities, the Charter would, Trudeau believes, strengthen Canadians' sometimes fragile sense of community. In his own words,

> [T]he Canadian Charter was a new beginning for the Canadian nation: it sought to strengthen the country's unity by basing the sovereignty of the Canadian people on a set of values common to all, and in particular on the notion of equality among all Canadians.
>
> Clearly, the very adoption of a constitutional charter is in keeping with the purest liberalism, according to which members of civil society enjoy certain fundamental inalienable rights and cannot be deprived of them by any collectivity (state or government) or on behalf of any collectivity (nation, ethnic group, religious group or other). (1990, 363)

Precisely the problem!, respond Quebec nationalists. The Charter enshrines a universalist vision of liberalism that denies the possibility of citizens belonging to Canada in different ways, through their membership in communities like Quebec, the Mohawk nation, or the Inuit people. They are understandably more comfortable with the communitarian liberalism of Charles Taylor. But Trudeau's vision of community, though unpopular with Quebec nationalists, is certainly more in tune with the political tradition of English-speaking Canada than Taylor's communitarian arguments about deep diversity.

CONCLUSION

Pierre Elliot Trudeau was a rarity in Canadian politics: an intellectual who acquired the opportunity to put into practice the ideas that he had developed during a lifetime of studying, writing, and teaching about politics and the law. He is widely thought of as Canada's "philosopher-king," a characterization that Trudeau seemed to welcome. His critics – and they are many – observe that the Trudeau who wrote *Quebec on the Eve of the Asbestos Strike* and who was an editor and contributor to the anti-establisment

Cité libre was not the Trudeau who invoked the War Measures Act, twice brought in wage controls, and presided over federal intrusions into areas of provincial jurisdiction that he railed against before joining the Liberal Party. The "king," they argue, abandoned the ideas and principles of the "philosopher" once in power. That Trudeau made compromises dictated by the discipline and constraints of governing and maintaining power is undeniable and unsurprising. At the same time he always remained faithful to the core values of his political philosophy.

At the heart of this philosophy is the primacy of individual freedom. Like Taylor, Trudeau rejected out of hand the idea that freedom involved the mere absence of constraint on individual action. The state, he believed, had a crucial role to play in addressing inequalities that undermined real freedom of choice. Moreover, Trudeau did not believe that all individual choices were equally worthy from a moral point of view. It is clear from his writings that he agreed with Taylor's argument that choices should be measured against a sort of moral horizon and that it is a person's ability to make enlightened choices, aware of the needs and welfare of others, that constitutes true freedom. Where Trudeau and Taylor part ways is in how each conceives of this moral horizon.

We already have seen that, for Taylor, personal dignity and the opportunity to experience genuine freedom cannot exist apart from the communal identity(ies) that invest a person's life and choices with meaning. Communal attachments loom large on his moral horizon. But in the case of Trudeau, personal dignity and the experience of meaningful freedom depend on the individual choosing and acting in ways that take account of society and the public good and – this is the key difference from Taylor – *overcoming* the ascriptive ties of community. Trudeau views communal identities with some suspicion. He certainly believes them to be morally inferior to the idea of the individual in society, a sort of collective identity that bridges ethnic, language, religious, and other more limited group identities.

As prime minister of Canada and, even after his departure from Ottawa, an influential combatant in Canada's constitutional debates, Trudeau demonstrated time and again his unflinching rationalist attachment to a political order founded on universal values and rights and his deep enmity toward the most powerful of modern communal identities, ethnicity-based nationalism. His insistence that language rights should be personal rather than territorial and his championing of the Charter as a means for generating a common civic identification among Canadians of all regions and groups were fully consistent with the political philosophy that he held throughout his adult life. In the end, for better or for worse, his ideas cut deep and enduring grooves across Canada's political landscape.

CHAPTER EIGHT

Six Influential Canadians

In the division of labour that characterizes intellectual life there are innovators – those who acquire original insights; scholars and researchers who evaluate and preserve the insights; communicators and educators who hand on the intellectual tradition; and citizens whose lives are enriched by deeper understanding and renewed public debate. We have focused on six innovators. Their careers have followed different paths and their forms of *engagement* have ranged from iconoclast to advisor to prime minister. What they have in common, however, is a passion for understanding the human condition – both locally and universally – and a desire to make a difference in the lives of their fellow citizens.

The four Quebec thinkers discussed here have spent most of their adult lives in Montreal and witnessed firsthand the struggles over language, identity, and the status of Quebec that have been at the heart of the Canadian experience. They are members of generations who lived in the Quebec of *la grande noirceur,* the years during which the unholy alliance of the church, American capital, and the Union Nationale held the province in a stranglehold that prevented the social, economic, and political reforms being undertaken elsewhere from making inroads in Quebec. All four were exposed to many of the same intellectually formative influences within the progressive wing of Catholicism – though Taylor did not attend a *collège classique* – whose voice was heard in forums like *Esprit* and whose leading intellectual figures were Emmanuel Mounier and Jacques Maritain. Besides experiencing a very similar early education, the three French Quebecers Laurendeau, Trudeau, and Rioux spent a period of their early adulthood in Paris – Laurendeau before the Second World War and Trudeau and Rioux immediately afterwards. They witnessed the excesses and injustices inflicted on Europe in the name of nationalism. In Laurendeau's words, "In Europe the homeland has demanded too many great sacrifices that led to the impoverishment of nations" (1952, 211, our translation). Yet it must be said that they drew starkly different conclusions from the common European experience.

A conviction that social, economic, and political reforms needed to be undertaken in Quebec and Canada runs like a unifying thread through the writings and lives of these four Quebecers. They have all been political activists in their various ways, seeking both truth and justice, as they understood these contentious matters, through their actions as well as their words. Their contribution to their times, intellectually and politically, is in the tradition of the French *intellectuels engagés*, like Malraux, Sartre, Aron, Levi-Strauss and others. One struggles to find their exact counterparts in English Canada. (Of course, Taylor can be claimed by English Canada, but it is difficult to imagine him having the same passionate interest in Quebec, language issues, and Quebec nationalism, or the same intellectual influence on these matters, if he had spent his career at the University of British Columbia or the University of Toronto, instead of McGill University.) Although English Canada has not been without its *grands penseurs* whose work has left clear imprints on the country, the tradition of the public intellectual seems to have shallower roots than in Quebec. Instead, the contributions of university-based intellectuals are usually channelled through royal commissions and other bureaucratic contrivances.[1]

Harold Innis and George Grant clearly are not English Canada's counterpart to this Quebec group. But they do stand apart, nonetheless. This is true for Innis because of the enduring and multidisciplinary impact of his research, his lasting if indirect influence on the direction and parameters of political discussion and debate in English Canada, and his academic leadership in the development of the social sciences. He preceded the other five thinkers discussed here by a generation or more. Moreover, as the only economist in the group, his thinking was shaped fundamentally by economic questions. His investigations sought understanding on a broad geo-political scale, including Canada's place within a series of empires (French, British, and American), and the influence this had on political and social structures and patterns of economic and regional development.

Grant, like Innis, was fascinated by the impact on society of modern technology, and the implications for Canada of the shift from political and economic dependency within the British Empire to a similar position within the American. Grant is especially noteworthy because both his ideas and the forceful and eloquent manner in which he presented them were unusually compelling and resonant beyond academic circles. Unlike most of his English-speaking academic colleagues and contemporaries, Grant was committed to the role of public intellectual and embraced it with gusto. His dramatic message tapped into English Canada's deep well of ambivalence about the meaning and impact of continental integration for Canadian culture, identity, and independence. And both Innis and Grant (along with another prominent Canadian thinker not profiled here – Marshall McLuhan) thought more deeply and intensely than others about the implications for Canada, for Western civilization, and indeed for the whole of humanity, of rapid, pervasive, and continuous technological change.

Of the four Quebec intellectuals whose work we have considered, three have had an important influence outside their home province. Since the 1960s it has been unthinkable that one could seriously discuss issues involving language rights, national unity, Canadian identity, and Quebec without confronting the ideas of Pierre Trudeau. André Laurendeau, editor for years of French Canada's most influential newspaper, *Le Devoir,* and one of the co-commissioners of the B & B Commission, projected his ideas and arguments well beyond his province and language community. Taylor's influence has been greatest in defining a communitarian politics of the left and as an intellectual guiding light for those groups critical of liberal-democratic capitalism. At the same time, he is widely read in both English Canada and Quebec, with his views often cited on matters relating to nationalism, language, Quebec, and reform of Canada's constitution.[2]

No similar claim of cross-cultural influence can be made for Innis and Grant.[3] Neither has had a significant influence on intellectual or political debates in French-speaking Quebec. The primary intellectual concerns addressed in their respective works – such as the economic and cultural impact on a peripheral Canada of larger empires (especially the United States), or the essential nature and character of modern technological society – have been for the most part secondary considerations for Quebec intellectuals and politicians, where the debate has tended to focus intensely on Quebec society and the Quebec-Canada relationship.

As befits thinkers of the first rank, all six individuals considered here have grappled with the fundamental issues of political life – the nature of individual freedom, the claims of the community on the individual, the character of the good society, and the conditions needed to ensure individual dignity. What we find is a broad consensus on the importance of freedom, equality, and community, but significant disagreements over the nature of these "goods." The analysis undertaken here allows us to draw comparisons between them, not only in terms of their abstract thinking about these goods (and the relationship between them), but also their role both in defining and shaping the debate over a number of key "issue clusters" that have been central to the broader political agenda and to Canadian political discourse. Thus, the foundational principle of human freedom or liberty has involved, among other things, questions of individual rights and the law, the design and operation of social and political institutions, and the relationship between state and society. The search for equality and social justice raises concerns related to capitalism and its economic and social effects, the place and status of ethnic or national minorities, colonialism and dependency, as well as regional inequality. The idea of community informs other debates: about nationalism (both Canadian and Québécois) and national unity, issues of identity and group rights, Canada's relationship with the United States, and provincial autonomy.

FREEDOM

The problem of freedom, seriously considered, must always be framed in relation to the nature of human dignity and the necessary claims of the community on the individual. None of the thinkers whose ideas we have examined would dissent from this claim. Nor does any of the six have a positive assessment of American-style individualism which, they all to varying degrees believe, ends up diminishing and denying individual freedom for society's less privileged elements by failing to provide them with the conditions necessary to meaningfully exercise free choice. At the same time, freedom is trivialized by implicitly treating all choices as equally deserving of protection. Rather, all six Canadian thinkers exhibit skepticism about the relationship of free market capitalism to human freedom. Freedom as mere freedom from interference – the right to be left alone and to do one's own thing – or what is referred to by its critics as the negative conception of freedom, leaves them unimpressed. Instead, all would agree that genuine freedom involves individual choice and action exercised against moral horizons. But what horizons?

Innis's view of freedom was shaped by his Anglo-Canadian heritage, by his economics training and research, and by his materialist analysis of Canadian and world history. The former gave Innis an understanding of the importance of stable, well-functioning political and social institutions to the enjoyment of individual freedom. In the Whig liberal tradition of Hume and Burke, Innis believed freedom was a function of historical and cultural conditions, the result of certain customs, conventions and institutions that evolve over a long period of time. It is the balance and stability produced by a certain kind of society which produces the conditions for human freedom. The greatest long-term threat to this freedom comes from disruption of this societal balance and stability, and the civil culture and autonomous institutions (protected spheres of non-interference such as parliaments, courts, common law, universities) which sustain it. The main source of this disruption is the tendency toward elite control over technology, wielded through large scale organizations (military, corporate, bureaucratic) which produces "monopolies of knowledge." This in turn leads to a concentration of social power and the construction of a form of ideological hegemony that suppresses freedom of thought and inquiry. In the modern era, the mechanization of knowledge is accelerating this tendency, undermining the social and cultural conditions that sustain individual freedom.

Innis is perhaps closest to Trudeau in his adherence to liberalism's focus on the individual, although Innis is much more suspicious of the long-term implications for individual freedom of the modern bureaucratic state. However, both Innis and Trudeau are pessimistic about the prospects for individual freedom in a society where ethnic nationalism is strong, and in particular where the state becomes the focus of nationalist feeling. Trudeau, following Maritain, believes that society, in which "personal consciousness retains priority ...

and social relations proceed from the voluntary determination of human persons" (1952, 4) involves a system of human relationships that is higher and morally superior to national ties and other communal associations. The latter are normal and inevitable, given that they are rooted in nature. But they do not permit the individual to experience true freedom, based as they are on nature rather than personal conscience and the voluntary determination of persons. Moreover, because freedom and human dignity are inextricably linked in Trudeau's philosophy, dignity can only be experienced by "man-in-society." It is not a quality of "man-in-community."

Although Rioux and Laurendeau were exposed to the same Catholic personalism that so influenced the thinking of Trudeau, they clearly did not take to heart the disdain in which prominent personalist thinkers like Maritain and Delos held nationalism. Like Taylor and Grant, Rioux and Laurendeau have no difficulty reconciling nationalism and a state based on the national principle with respect for individual freedom. This is because all four believe that true freedom is only realizable in a context that nurtures and affirms those communal associations and identities that give a person's life dignity. They all agree that freedom is not its own justification – that is, freedom as the absence of restraint – but that it needs to be invested with some moral significance that derives from the relationship between the individual's actions and choices, on the one hand, and the common good on the other. Their conception of this common good is one that allows nationalism a much more elevated status than is acceptable to either Trudeau or Innis.

In the case of each of the three French Quebecers, there is a key to their particular understandings of freedom. For Laurendeau it is his belief that individual freedom and full personal development are only possible within the larger context of the nation. Insofar as the nation is the community that bequeaths meaning to one's life through a common culture, it must be recognized and nurtured. Otherwise, freedom and individual dignity become impossible.

Rioux would agree, but his view of freedom has its own distinctive twist. In Rioux's case alienation is the chief obstacle to human freedom, an argument that has strong echoes of the early Marx. The emancipation of the nation is a necessary step toward the emancipation of the individual. It is, however, not a sufficient step. All forms of alienation must be overcome, which means that all structures and ideological systems that prevent people from experiencing their own possibilities, whether this alienation be cultural, economic, or political, must be eliminated before the autonomy of the individual and true freedom become possible. Consequently, a politically independent Quebec would not guarantee freedom to Quebecers, although Rioux is infinitely more sanguine than Trudeau that the cause of individual freedom would not be set back by Quebec independence. On the contrary, the alienation that derives from the domination of one nation by another is, Rioux maintains, one of the most serious obstacles to human freedom, and so the national emancipation of Quebec is a crucial step toward the personal emancipation of Quebecers.

The key to Trudeau's view of freedom is his conception of society. While recognizing the inevitability and even, in some circumstances, the salutary nature of human associations based on ties of blood, ethnicity, and culture, Trudeau considers these associations to be morally inferior to those which are based on personal choice that is indifferent to these communal bonds. Communities will always exist within political society, but political society should never be based on the ties of community. It is not one's identification with a communal group that gives life dignity and invests his actions with the moral significance of a truly free individual. Rather, Trudeau would say, it is only when the deterministic tug of such communal bonds has been overcome, and people live in a society in which their relations and obligations toward one another are based on reason and consent, that men and women may be said to be truly free. A state based on the national principle is, for Trudeau, the antithesis of a free society and an affront to human dignity.

Taylor's view of freedom shares some of its conceptual architecture with Trudeau's – in particular the debt to Kant in conceiving of freedom as virtuous action that can only occur within the moral order that is society. Where they part company is in Taylor's insistence on the importance of authenticity in determining the moral character of individual freedom. By authenticity Taylor means the distinctively human qualities that are affirmed through the exercise of free will, qualities that necessarily link the individual to larger communities. Taylor's qualified sympathy for nationalist aspirations, including Quebec's language policies since the 1970s and constitutional recognition of Quebec as a *société distincte*, derives from his belief that the collective purposes associated with nationalism may enrich the dignity of individuals and be part of the moral horizon that gives truly human meaning to their lives. The key to achieving freedom is authenticity, and authenticity requires opportunities to affirm and experience the public meanings of our lives. Nationalism may provide these opportunities, says Taylor.

Grant's thinking on freedom shares much with Taylor; both are critics of modernity and liberalism. But Grant, like Innis, is much more pessimistic about the threat to freedom posed by the reordering of social relations and the changes in societal values (and even morality) that are necessary in order to accommodate the continuous, rapid, and pervasive change that is the hallmark of modern technological society. Grant believes that the systematic removal of all institutional and cultural barriers to change – in other words, "total freedom" – will ultimately undermine that very human freedom, the expansion of which is cited as the justification for further change. It does so because it removes all restraints on a self-perpetuating "will to mastery" that infects Western civilization and becomes increasingly amoral as well as socially, culturally, and environmentally destructive. Regrettably, as the assertion of individual choice and rights becomes the prime directive for society, all other cultural traditions, mores, social obligations, and spiritual values become secondary and expendable.

EQUALITY

All six thinkers considered here are social progressives, although their degree of commitment to a redistributive ethic ranges from Trudeau, Innis, and Laurendeau at the moderate end, to Taylor, Grant, and Rioux at the more radical end. All six have written and spoken out against various forms of imperialism and colonialism, whether cultural, economic, or military. None has any time for American-style egalitarianism, influenced by the idea of the frontier and the powerful current of rugged individualism that continues to occupy an important place in the American psyche. Instead of rugged individualism, they see bonds of social obligation. In addition, the four Quebecers were part of the political and intellectual opposition to the unholy alliance that dominated Quebec politics under Maurice Duplessis.

These similarities should not be allowed to obscure the important differences between them. As in the case of their thoughts on freedom, Trudeau and Innis stand apart somewhat from the others on the question of equality. They adopt the more traditionally liberal position of focusing on *individuals* as the possessors of rights, not *groups*. They emphasize the need to liberate and enable individuals to fulfill their potential, rather than communities, social classes, or whole societies.

Having thus set Innis and Trudeau apart, it immediately becomes necessary to distinguish between them, for they are very different from one another. Innis's ideas about equality are manifested in his abiding concern with balance, proportion, and moderation, and his analysis of the dangerous biases inherent in monopoly, empire, and centre-periphery relations. He detested and feared the consequences of gross inequalities of wealth, power, and knowledge, whether between individuals, social groups, regions, or nations, and sought to demonstrate the corrosive and counterproductive effects of such inequalities for all concerned. Complete equality was neither possible nor to be wished for, but the wisdom and virtue of removing the obstacles that hindered or blocked individuals from pursuing the development of their own capacities and potentials is a repeated theme that runs through Innis's thinking. So are his dark forebodings about Canada's future within the American empire, which exhibits little regard for balance and moderation or concern about the social and geographic concentration of power.

As for Trudeau, it may seem odd to claim that he has always maintained that individuals possess rights only as individuals, never by virtue of their membership in a group. This, after all, is a person who championed official bilingualism and minority language rights throughout his adult life, whose government brought in Canada's first official policy on multiculturalism, and who successfully navigated constitutional entrenchment of the Charter of Rights and Freedoms, which in various ways recognizes and protects group rights, through the shoals of considerable provincial opposition. However, Trudeau has consistently maintained the position that individuals are deserving of equal treatment because of the equal dignity of all persons; dignity that is undermined when equality rights are guaranteed to communities as such, rather than to individuals. The regime of official bilingualism instituted under Trudeau accords language rights to individual members of the French- and English-speaking language communities, wherever they live in Canada, rather than to the communities on a territorial basis as is done in Belgium and Switzerland. He has always been adamant that conferring special rights on ethnic, linguistic, religious, or other groups, or somehow assigning them distinct status, is a denial of human dignity. His unflinching resolve on this score is usually attributed to what is called his rationalism – his excessive rationalism, critics would say. In fact, however, the more important cause is Trudeau's belief that personal dignity is not anchored to one's relationship to a community, but rather to an internalized sense of what is virtuous, a sense that can only be realized at what he believes is the morally higher plane of social organization that is society.

Laurendeau co-headed the royal commission that recommended the regime of linguistic equality that was instituted under the first Trudeau government. His views on the equality of French and English in Canada are not, however, in sync with Trudeau's. When Laurendeau turns his thoughts toward equality, it is usually the equality between Canada's *two founding peoples* that concerns him. He believed that the full equality of the French and English nations within Canada was a precondition for realizing individual equality. So long as the two nations remained unequal in their ability to participate in the political, economic, and social life of the country, and in their opportunities to express their cultural uniqueness, the equality of individuals would remain illusory. This is not so different from Trudeau, except that Trudeau would not cast the issue in terms of the equality of nations. Moreover, Laurendeau was far more sympathetic than Trudeau to the nationalist-independentist movement, and far more likely to look to the Quebec government as the only reliable guardian of the French nation within Canada.

Rioux goes a long step beyond Laurendeau in maintaining that independence for Quebec is a necessary precondition for the equality of nations that Laurendeau always hoped could be achieved within Canadian federalism. Independence, Rioux acknowledges, would not guarantee the emergence of a new society based on social democratic principles – how often has national liberation resulted in the replacement of one ethnic elite by another? – but it would be a step toward overcoming one of the chief obstacles to the creation of a truly egalitarian society, namely, cultural and economic domination. Rioux was also firmly convinced of the need for the devolution of authority and self-government to regions and local groups of citizens. "Once our collective emancipation is realized," he writes, "we will have to initiate policies that recognize our internal diversity" (1979:208, our translation). Rioux's vision of what an emancipated society would look like resembles Taylor's more than either Trudeau's or Laurendeau's.

Taylor and Grant offer a similar perspective on the question of equality. Both deliver scathing critiques of a capitalist economic system fuelled by greed and materialism. Both link equality to community, specifically the link between loss of community and growing inequality. A positive role for the state, whereby it becomes the instrument for collective goals that promote the dignity of all, acting to restrain private greed in the name of social good, cannot be sustained where an ideology of unfettered individualism and glorification of the free market enfeebles the state and undermines citizen identification with the fate of the community. Yet this, say Taylor and Grant, is exactly the result that can be expected in Canada from the increasingly pervasive cultural and economic influence of the United States. Extending equality in Canadian society, rather than fostering ever-greater inequality, depends on counterbalancing the capitalist ethic with a clearly defined ethic of community.

This close relationship posited between equality and community helps to explain the strong support offered by both Taylor and Grant to Canadian *and* Québécois nationalism. Here their views converge with Laurendeau and Rioux. All wish to see a more self-aware English-speaking Canada extending recognition and equality of status to the Québécois nation. While Taylor makes this the cornerstone of his proposed solution to Canada's vexing national unity question, Grant views it in terms of a cross-national alliance aimed at checking and delaying the seemingly inevitable assimilation of both English- and French-speaking Canadians into an American-centred melting pot of cultural sameness.

COMMUNITY

As we have seen, community is an important concept for all six thinkers, but not always for the same reasons or in the same way. For political economist Innis, the notion of community, and its place in his thinking, is somewhat different from the others. Community is a seminal if not often acknowledged presence in Innis's researches and writings. Indeed, Canada's existence as a natural political and economic community, rather than an artificial creation in defiance of geography and history, was the primary idea and line of argument developed by Innis and others in the "Laurentian School" of political economists and historians. In general terms, Innis (and this is certainly true of Grant as well) was convinced that one could only understand economic and social reality, and the unfolding of history, through sweeping interpretations that encompassed whole civilizations and spanned centuries-long epochs. This grand, holistic approach naturally creates a focus on the fates of whole communities, operating as functioning units within a larger set of relationships. Such relationships between communities – especially between centres and peripheries, metropoles and their hinterlands – is the primary subject matter of Innisian political economy.

Innis brought to this subject matter an overriding concern for *balance* in human relations, and his analysis of the long-term negative consequences of monopoly and centralization convinced him of the crucial importance of gaining and protecting Canadian independence vis à vis the American metropole. It also led him to strongly defend the need to preserve provincial autonomy from the centralizing tendencies of the federal bureaucracy, and to clarify and highlight the distinct needs of regional economies as against the policy preferences of the industrial and financial core in central Canada. In each case, this reflected Innis's recognition of the importance of economically vital, politically self-governing communities to the quality and sustainability of the social institutions, as well as to the individual freedoms, within those communities.

Grant also sounded the alarm about the erosion of a sovereign, distinct Canadian community, as well as the need to protect the autonomy of provincial communities, because he believed that genuine human freedom was possible only in the context of a social order and a community undergirded by traditions and institutions that provided both limits and supports for that freedom. It is through identification with things that are their own, argues Grant, and participation within the particular communities to which they belong, that individuals are able "to grasp what is good" for both themselves and their fellow citizens. For most, this is the essential foundation for partaking in a more universal good – justice, charity, loyalty, respect for the equal worth and dignity of every person, and for Grant of course, love of God. In other words, the particular cannot be sacrificed or undervalued in favour of the general, a "crime" of which Grant accused (in no uncertain terms, in typical

Grantian style) true-believer liberals, including such notables as Pierre Trudeau.

It is especially with the four Quebec thinkers, however, that the idea of community takes centre stage and generates intense, principled arguments. In the introductory chapter to this book we discussed the concept of self-determination and the success of Quebec nationalists since the 1960s in convincing many English-speaking intellectuals that Quebec constitutes a nation, a colonized society, and that it has an inherent right to determine its own future. This bundle of premises involves an idea of community that has surfaced in various forms over the years, from Canada as a community of communities, through "two nations" theories of Confederation, special status for Quebec within Canadian federalism, to sovereignty-association and outright political independence for Quebec. It is an idea of community that sees the national community, defined by common bonds of language, history, and mutual identification, as a natural – some would go so far as to say desirable – basis on which to build a state. The communitarian philosophies of Laurendeau, Rioux, and Taylor (and also, it might be said, Grant) all provide intellectual support for this idea of community.

Although their arguments are rather different, Rioux and Taylor both see communal identities as potentially liberating for the individual and as an increasingly necessary form of insulation against the alienation (Rioux) or atomization (Taylor) experienced by modern people in a global economic-cum-cultural system that flattens out the uniqueness of cultures and offers instead an unsatisfying sameness of experience and consciousness. They differ, however, on the question of Quebec independence. Taylor believes that the communal aspirations of *les Québécois* can be accommodated through reforms to Canadian federalism, which at a minimum would involve constitutional recognition of Quebec as a distinct society, although a more durable reconciliation of the two solitudes would probably have to be based on implementation of the asymmetrical federalism implied by Taylor's notion of deep diversity. Rioux insists that nothing short of political independence for Quebec can overcome the oppression and alienation that he believes are inevitable within the federalist straitjacket. Rioux views Quebec as a society that has been deformed and stunted by colonization, and clearly accepts the analogy between Quebec and colonized peoples of the underdeveloped world. He is confident that Quebec independence need not degenerate into an intolerant ethnic nationalism, but that smaller collectivities like aboriginal communities and even the English minority in Quebec can all experience a sense of belonging to a pluralistic Quebec society that allows them to affirm their collective identities within an independent Quebec.

Laurendeau's idea of community is in the tradition of Henri Bourassa, the founder and first editor of *Le Devoir*, of which Laurendeau was in turn editor. Like Bourassa, he emphasized the cultural aspects of nationhood and insisted on the special role of Quebec for the protection of the language and traditions of French Canada. Laurendeau always rejected the view that Quebec should be treated as a province like the others, recognizing that demographics and the assimilationist pressures on francophone minorities outside Quebec resulted in a situation where Quebec was unavoidably, in a real sense, the national state of French Canadians. Moreover, Laurendeau did not hesitate to speak of *la société québécoise*, by which he meant the ensemble of institutions and relations inspired by the French language and common culture of Quebec. Together, these notions of Quebec as the national state for Canadian francophones and of Quebec as a distinct society would provide the architecture for moderate nationalist thinking about reform of Canadian federalism. It is easy to see the linkages between Laurendeau's thought and the concepts of *statut particulier* and *société distincte* that have led to many political debates since the 1960s.

These beliefs set Laurendeau apart from Trudeau, although in other respects their views on Canadian dualism and the equal status of the two language communities within federal institutions were broadly similar. But at the end of the day Laurendeau is a Quebec nationalist – albeit with a foot in *le nationalisme canadien-français* of Henri Bourassa – whereas Trudeau most adamantly is not. Trudeau rejects the notion of special constitutional status for Quebec, seeing in it the elevation of communal identity to a level he believes threatening to minority rights and corrosive of human dignity.

Dignity is the rub. It is the point at which Trudeau parts company from Laurendeau and all others who are sympathetic toward Quebec nationalism. For whereas the nationalists insist that individual dignity and a good life require the experience of living in a community and the recognition of one's communal identity through social and political institutions, Trudeau is able to imagine personal dignity that is not anchored to one's communal identity, but which transcends that identity. It is the transcendence that gives one's actions and life dignity, argues Trudeau. Again, the key is to understand the distinction that Trudeau makes between community and society. Communities defined by bonds of language, ethnicity, culture, and history are, he insists, morally inferior to societies in which the bonds of civic life transcend communal identities. In a very real sense Trudeau remains perhaps the last prominent Canadian spokesman for the idea of civic nationalism, an idea which Taylor argues has seen its day and is unsuited to the modern yearning for authenticity. The communitarian vision elaborated in different ways by Laurendeau, Rioux, and Taylor has been ascendant in recent years. Time will tell if this is merely a swing of the intellectual pendulum, or whether it presages a profound reconfiguration of the Canadian experiment in reconciling communal differences.

CONCLUSION

Through their own praxis (that is, the practical application of their ideas within the political and social arenas in which they participated) and through the influence of their ideas on others, each of the thinkers discussed in this book has left an enduring legacy. Each has made a difference

Innis, the academic iconoclast who was acutely aware of "having insight into much and power over nothing" dedicated his life to creating and developing a distinctively Canadian approach – the staples approach – to understanding the country's historical development, while simultaneously helping to establish and defend the infrastructure and the scholarly standards of autonomous, university-based social science research in Canada.

Grant, the unorthodox, contrary-minded social critic, railed against the gathering gloom, as he perceived it, and challenged the basic assumptions and comfortable nostrums of the Canadian Establishment and its functionaries. He did this not so much with a view to actually reversing the direction of things – which to him seemed implacably set – but to lament what had been lost, to vigorously critique the status quo, and to raise the alarm about the future toward which modern society was moving.

Taylor, the philosopher *engagé* of Canada's nationalist left, has evolved from an angry young man of Canadian politics in the 1960s to one of the English-speaking world's most respected intellectuals.

His communitarianism attempts to refashion liberal thought in ways that place personal dignity, identity, and authenticity at centre stage. Unlike the more pessimistic Grant, Taylor has never given the impression, either through his work or his political involvement, that he believed himself to be a champion of lost causes.

Laurendeau, a politically-involved humanist, was deeply concerned with the management of diversity in Canada. His involvement took different forms, including party politics, journalism, and serving with one of Canada's most important royal commissions. Laurendeau's analyses were characterized by impressive foresight, and in many ways have been vindicated in societies throughout the developed world. In Canada, however, his ideas have been overshadowed by Trudeau's approach of downplaying deep diversity in favour of encouraging a single Canadian identity.

Rioux, one of Quebec's most prominent left-wing intellectuals, was inspired by the realm of possibilities that he saw in small villages, towns, and hinterlands. He was always critical of centralising and imperialist forces, and imagined alternatives that he believed would alleviate injustices and unfair treatment. The quest for equality between social classes, national communities, and peoples was a major driving force behind his philosophy of life and politics.

Trudeau, at the other end of the spectrum from the monastic scholar Innis, had the opportunity to put his ideas into practice and to reshape Canadian political institutions. This he did, presiding over the passage of the Official Languages Act (1969), Ottawa's response to the October Crisis (1970), and the 1982 Constitution Act, including the Charter of Rights and Freedoms. Finally, his public intervention may have been a decisive factor in the 1990 defeat of the Meech Lake Accord. When Trudeau died in the autumn of 2000 there was a national sense of loss. This may have had less to do with his legacy of policies and institutions (not all of which have been popular with many Canadians and Québécois) than with the feeling that Canada had lost its "philosopher-king," a rare enough creature in any society, but particularly so in Canadian political life.

All of these men have made a lasting and indelible impression on the firmament of Canadian political thought. Their contributions continue to resonate in Canadian and Quebec society and politics, and doubtless will do so for generations to come.

Notes

CHAPTER ONE

1 For a solid analysis on the rethinking that took place among establishment politicians and bureaucrats, see Owram 1986.
2 For a masterful account of royal commissions and their role in the policy-learning, see Bradford 1998.

CHAPTER TWO

1 The one main exception to Innis's suspicion about direct collaboration with government was his service on the 1935 Nova Scotia Royal Commission of Economic Inquiry. Even so, on this occasion Innis's independent streak was quite evident. He submitted his own separate report rather than simply endorsing or "signing on" to the Commission Report itself.

CHAPTER THREE

1 Panitch 1995, 152.
2 On his growing understanding of the relationship between "the two sources from which all our wisdom comes, Greek philosophy and biblical religion," Grant gave much credit to his conversations with departmental colleague and Oxford contemporary, the Hegelian philosopher James Doull (Christian 1993, 192).

3 Grant's experience of modern technological society both attracted and repelled him, "but he thought that if he were ever to see the direction in which it was moving, he had to experience modernity in its fullest. Consequently he felt isolated in Nova Scotia and he began to think seriously that he should leave Dalhousie" (Christian 1993, 196).

4 Grant was giving serious consideration to a position at Claremont University in California. McMaster's offer left him grateful that he could rule out going to the United States. "It means a great deal to myself and my wife and children not to have to become Americans" (as quoted in Christian 1993, 210).

5 In the 1962 election, Grant followed up this intellectual contribution by working hard for the new party (the NDP) as campaign agent in his home riding. However, this formal party connection lasted only a year or so, after which he established contact with other, more radical critics of North American civilization: the New Left and especially the growing and increasingly politicized student movement on university campuses (Christian 1993, 212, 214).

6 Grant had pleaded with the NDP's leader, Tommy Douglas, not to vote against the government on this issue, and when it did so, he concluded they were no more than "a vacuous extension of the Liberals" whom he regretted having had anything to do with (Christian 1993, 241).

7 Because Grant, like Innis, thought in terms of empires, the popular embrace by Canadians of technological progress and its accompanying notion of freedom "made inevitable Canada's absorption into the American empire" (Taylor 1982, 141).

8 Grant explores the relationship between abortion and the liberal conception of freedom in a number of essays in the 1980s, including "The Case Against Abortion" 1981; and "The Triumph of the Will" 1988.

9 Grant became convinced of the importance of higher education for democracy through his involvement in adult education, which began in 1943 when he was hired by the Canadian Association for Adult Education, and continued in various forms for the rest of his life (Christian 1993, 94).

10 Grant cited two purposes to human existence: to live together well in communities and to think. The "tyranny" produced by the monolithic apparatus constructed in the pursuit of technological control (mastery over nature) "is the greatest political foe of human

excellence. It denies both the chief ends of man – living together well and thinking" (Christian and Grant 1988, 99).

CHAPTER FOUR

1 Guy Laforest is of the view that, while Trudeau's ideas have dominated the Canadian political scene, it is Laurendeau's conceptualization of communities that is succeeding at the international level. (cf. Laforest's intervention before the Annual Meeting of the Association of Canadian Philosophers, Brock University, 1 June 1996)
2 This term is borrowed from Pierre Anctil.
3 On the conscription crisis, see André Laurendeau 1962.
4 See, for instance, *Le Devoir,* 18 October 1943 which reported radio coverage done on 16 and 17 October.
5 The distinction made by Michael Behiels (1985) between neo-nationalism and *Cité libre* liberalism appears to be exaggerated based on Oliver's rendering of the situation prevailing at the time (cf. to Oliver's *The Passionate Debate* completed in 1956 but published in 1991 in the aftermath of the Meech Lake failure).
6 See Léon Dion's portrait of Maurice Lamontagne in *Québec 1945–2000: Les intellectuels et le temps de Duplessis*, tome II, 1993, 179–83.
7 For a discussion of nationalist versus neo-nationalist tendencies, one can refer to Michael Behiels 1985 among others.
8 The best example of this is provided by his work *Lament for a Nation* 1965.

CHAPTER FIVE

1 For instance, one can refer to Rioux's condemnation of Trudeau's actions with respect to the 1980 referendum: *Pour prendre publiquement congé de quelques salauds* 1981.
2 Rioux attributes the origins of this concept to the German notion of *Aufhebung* used by Hegel and Marx when they referred to the need to understand contradictions and dysfunctions underlying capitalism (Rioux 1990a, 104–5).
3 On this period, refer to Duchastel 1981, 115–19.
4 One can see some affinities between the works of Herbert Marcuse and Rioux.

5 Rioux made his interpretation of culture even more complex by adding two other levels: a fourth level that he labelled "cultural formation" and a fifth one that he called "the space of man" – *le lieu de l'homme* (see respectively Rioux 1984, 38–40 and Rioux and Crean 1980, 47–8).
6 For debates confronting Quebec sociologists at the time, see Renée B. Dandurand 1992, 49–57.
7 *Possibles*, a journal committed to Quebec's independence, was given a socialist orientation and was committed to the articulation of an *autogestion* project (self-management) for Quebec (Fournier 1992, 197–8).
8 Cf. Marcel Rioux, Hélène Loiselle, François Loranger, Claude Jutra, Léon Bellefleur, Laurent Bouchard, and Gérald Godin 1975.
9 This work is part of a collaborative effort between Marcel Rioux and Susan Crean in which each took the leadership to write to their respective political communities concerning how they conceive a way out of the constitutional crisis. Rioux was responsible for writing *Deux pays pour vivre: un plaidoyer* (with Crean's input) whereas Crean wrote *Two Nations* (with Rioux's input). In this monograph, references will be made only to *Deux pays pour vivre: un plaidoyer.*

CHAPTER SEVEN

1 Maritain is one of the philosophers mentioned most often by Trudeau as having influenced his own thinking.
2 The Act has since been replaced by the *Emergency Powers Act.*
3 See James Laxer and Robert Laxer 1977; Gregory Baum and Duncan Cameron 1984; Leo Panitch and Donald Swartz 1985.
4 See, for instance, Mel Hurtig 1991.
5 Donald Smiley 1967.

CHAPTER EIGHT

1 For further development on this point, see Brooks and Gagnon 1988.
2 Although Rioux's work was made accessible to English readers thanks to the efforts of Susan Crean (see *Two Nations*, 1983), it is no doubt fair to say that his impact in English Canada has not been significant, especially in comparison with the other three. More important, if indirect, has been the impact that his ideas have had on the nationalist movement in Quebec.

3 It is true that Grant's seminal book, *Lament for a Nation*, was introduced and translated into French by Jacques-Yvan Morin under the title of *Est-ce la fin du Canada? Lamentations sur l'échec du nationalisme canadien*, Quebec, Hurtubise HMH, 1987, but this was over two decades after its original publication in English. Innis's work was even longer in gaining exposure. In a colloquium organized in 1997 by Charles Acland and William Buxton, and its subsequent publication *Harold Innis in the New Century: Reflections and Refractions*, two chapters try to explain why Innis's ideas were present in Quebec but not particularly influential.

Bibliography

Acland, Charles. 1999. "Histories of Places and Power: Innis in Canadian Cultural Studies." In Acland and Buxton 1999, 243–60.

Acland, Charles and William Buxton, eds. 1999. *Harold Innes in the New Century: Reflections and Refractions*. Montreal & Kingston: McGill-Queen's University Press.

Anctil, Pierre. 1988. *Le Devoir, les Juifs et l'immigration*. Québec: Institut québécois de recherche sur la culture.

– 1990. "Laurendeau et le grand virage identitaire de la Révolution tranquille." In Comeau and Beaudry 1990, 227–40.

Balthazar, Louis. 1990. "André Laurendeau, un artiste du nationalisme." In Comeau and Beaudry 1990, 169–78.

Baum, Gregory and Duncan Cameron, eds. 1984. *Ethics and Economics: Canada's Catholic Bishops on the Economic Crisis*. Toronto: Lorimer.

Behiels, Michael D. 1985. *Prelude to Québec's Quiet Revolution: Liberalism versus Neo-Nationalism, 1945–1960*. Montreal: McGill-Queen's University Press.

Berland, Jody. 1999. "Space at the Margins: Critical Theory and Colonial Spaces after Innis." In Acland and Buxton 1999, 281–308.

Berger, Carl. 1976. *The Writing of Canadian History: Aspects of English Canadian Historical Writing 1900–1970*. Toronto: Oxford University Press.

Bickerton, James. 1999. "Too Long in Exile: Innis and Maritime Political Economy." In Acland and Buxton 1999, 225–39.

Bourgault, Pierre. 1982. *Écrits polémiques 1960–1981: la politique.* Montréal: VLB éditeur.

Bradford, Neil. 1998. *Commissioning Ideas: Canadian National Policy Innovation in Comparative Perspective.* Toronto: Oxford University Press.

Brodie, Janine and Jane Jenson. 1989. *Crisis, Challenge and Change: Party and Class Revisited.* Ottawa: Carleton University Press.

Brooks, Stephen and Alain-G. Gagnon. 1988. *Social Scientists and Politics in Canada: Between Clerisy and Vanguard.* Montreal: Boréal.

Canada. Royal Commission on Bilingualism and Biculturalism. 1967. *Report of the Royal Commission on Bilingualism and Biculturalism,* General Introduction, Book 1: The Official Languages. Ottawa.

Carey, James. 1999. "Innis 'in' Chicago: Hope as the Sire of Discovery." In Acland and Buxton 1999, 81–104.

Christian, William. 1977. "Harold Innis as Political Theorist." *Canadian Journal of Political Science* 10, (March): 21–42.

– ed. 1980. *The Idea File of Harold Adams Innis.* Toronto: University of Toronto Press.

– 1993. *George Grant: A Biography.* Toronto: University of Toronto Press.

Christian, William and Sheila Grant, eds. 1998. *The George Grant Reader.* Toronto: University of Toronto Press.

Clark, S.D. 1981. "The Contribution of H.A. Innis to Canadian Scholarship." In Melody, Salter, and Heyer 1981, 27–36.

Clement, Wallace and Glen Williams. 1989. "Introduction." In Wallace Clement and Glen Williams, eds. *The New Canadian Political Economy.* Montreal & Kingston: McGill-Queen's University Press, 3–15.

Comeau, Paul-André. 1982. *Le bloc populaire, 1942–1948.* Montréal: Québec/Amérique.

– 1990. "Préface." In *Journal tenu pendant la Commission royale d'enquête sur le bilinguisme et le biculturalisme.* Montréal: VLB, Éditeur/Sepentrion.

Comeau, Robert and Lucille Beaudry, eds. 1990. *André Laurendeau: Un intellectuel d'ici.* Sillery: Les Presses de l'Université du Québec.

Commission d'enquête sur l'enseignement des arts au Québec (Commission Rioux). 1969. *Rapport.* 3 vols. Québec: L'Éditeur officiel du Québec.

Cooper, Barry. 1978. "A imperio usque ad imperium: The Political Thought of George Grant." In Schmidt 1978, 13–21.

Crean, Susan and Marcel Rioux. 1983. *Two Nations.* Toronto: Lorimer.

Creighton, Donald. 1981. "Harold Adams Innis: An Appraisal." In Melody, Salter, and Heyer 1981, 13–26.

Dandurand, Renée B. 1992. "Marcel Rioux et Fernand Dumont: deux penseurs québécois de la culture (1965–1985)." In Jacques Hamel et

Louis Maheu, eds. *Hommage à Marcel Rioux. Sociologie critique, création artistique et société contemporaine.* Montréal: Éditions Saint-Martin, 39–76.

Dansereau, Pierre. 1990. "André Laurendeau: les options réversibles." In Comeau and Beaudry 1990, 179–184.

Dion, Léon. 1973. "Québec and the Future of Canada." In Dale Thomson, ed. *Québec Society and Politics: Views from the Inside.* Toronto: McClelland and Stewart, 250–62.

– 1990. "André Laurendeau: un intellectuel engagé?" In Comeau and Beaudry 1990, 265–76.

– 2002. *Québec 1945–2000: Les intellectuels et le temps de Duplessis.* tome 2. Sainte-Foy: Les Presses de l'Université Laval.

Drache, Daniel. 1995. "Introduction: Celebrating Innis: The Man, the Legacy, and Our Future." In *Staples, Markets and Cultural Change,* (by Harold Innis.) Edited by Daniel Drache. Montreal & Kingston: McGill-Queen's University Press, xiii-lix.

Drache, Daniel and Wallace Clement. 1985. "Introduction: The Coming Age of Canadian Political Economy." In Daniel Drache and Wallace Clement, eds., *The New Practical Guide to Canadian Political Economy.* Toronto: James Lorimer and Company, ix-xxiv.

Duchastel, Jules. 1981. *Marcel Rioux. Entre l'utopie et la raison.* Montréal: Nouvelle Optique.

Dumont, Fernand. 1990. "De Laurendeau à l'intellectuel d'aujourd'hui." In Comeau and Beaudry 1990, 259–63.

Filion, Gérard. 1947. "La démission de M. Laurendeau." *Le Devoir,* 9 July.

Fournier, Marcel. 1992 ."Le sens du possible." In Jacques Hamel et Louis Maheu, eds., *Hommage à Marcel Rioux. Sociologie critique, création artistique et société contemporaine.* Montréal: Éditions Saint-Martin, 197–205.

Galbraith, John Kenneth. 1958. *The Affluent Society.* Boston: Houghton Mifflin.

Grant, George. 1965. *Lament for a Nation: The Defeat of Canadian Nationalism.* Toronto: McClelland and Stewart.

– 1969a. *Technology and Empire: Perspectives on North America.* Toronto: Anansi Press.

– 1969b. *Time as History.* Toronto: Canadian Broadcasting Corporation.

– 1981. "The Case Against Abortion." *Today Magazine,* 3 October: 12–13.

– 1985. *English-Speaking Justice.* Toronto: Anansi Press.

– 1988. "The Triumph of the Will." In Denyse O'Leary, ed. *The Issue of Life: A Christian Response to Abortion in Canada.* Burlington: Welch Publishing, 156–66.

Guillaume, Sylvie. 1990. "La transmission de l'héritage français: trois types de nationalisme canadien-français, 1913–1959." In *Québec Studies* 10 (Spring-Summer): 121–32.

Heyer, Paul. 1981. "Innis and the History of Communication: Antecedents, Parallels, and Unsuspected Biases." In Melody, Salter, and Heyer 1981, 247–60.

Horton, Donald J. 1992. *André Laurendeau: French Canadian Nationalist 1912–1968*. Toronto: Oxford University Press.

Hurtig, Mel. 1991. *The Betrayal of Canada*. Toronto: Stoddart.

Innis, Harold. 1936. "Discussion in the Social Sciences." *Dalhousie Review* 15 (January): 401–13.

– 1940. "Review of the Rowell-Sirois Report." *Canadian Journal of Economics and Political Science* 6: 562–71.

– 1946. *Political Economy in the Modern State*. Toronto: Ryerson Press.

– 1956a. *Essays in Canadian Economic History*. Ed. by Mary Q. Innis. Toronto: University of Toronto Press.

– 1956b. *The Fur Trade in Canada: An Introduction to Canadian Economic History*. (Orig. pub. 1930.) Toronto: University of Toronto Press.

– 1964a. *The Bias of Communication*. (Orig. pub. 1951.) Toronto: University of Toronto Press.

– 1964b. *The Cod Fisheries: The History of an International Economy*. (Orig. pub. 1940.) Toronto: University of Toronto Press.

King, William Lyon Mackenzie. 1918. *Industry and Humanity: A Study in the Principles of Underlying Reconstruction*. Toronto: T. Allen.

Kroker, Arthur. 1984. *Technology and the Canadian Mind: Innis/McLuhan/Grant*. Montreal: New World Perspectives.

Laforest, Guy. 1995. *Trudeau and the End of a Canadian Dream*. Montreal: McGill-Queen's University Press.

Laurendeau, André. 1952. "Y a-t-il une crise du nationalisme." *L'Action nationale* 40 (December): 205–25.

– 1962. *La crise de la conscription 1942*. Montréal: Les Éditions du jour.

– 1970. *Ces choses qui nous arrivent: Chronique des années 1961–1966*. Montréal: Éditions HMH.

– 1973. *André Laurendeau: Witness for Québec*. Essays selected and translated by Philip Stratford. Toronto: Macmillan of Canada.

– 1990. *Journal tenu pendant la Commission royale d'enquête sur le bilinguisme et le biculturalisme*. With a preface by Paul-André Comeau. Montréal: VLB, Éditeur/Sepentrion.

Laxer, James and Robert Laxer. 1977. *The Liberal Idea of Canada: Pierre Trudeau and the Question of Canada's Survival*. Toronto: Lorimer.

Levitt, Kari. 1970. *Silent Surrender: The Multinational Corporation in Canada*. Toronto: Macmillan of Canada.

Linteau, Paul-André, René Durocher, Jean-Claude Robert, François Ricard. 1986. *Histoire du Québec contemporain: Le Québec depuis 1930*. Montréal: Boréal.

Maritain, Jacques. 1952. *Man and the State*. Chicago: University of Chicago Press.

Melody, William, Liora Salter, and Paul Heyer. 1981. *Culture, Communication and Dependency: The Tradition of H.A. Innis*. Norwood, NJ: Ablex Publishing.

Millard, Gregory and Jane Forsey. 2001. "Technology and the Malaise of Modern Agency: Grant and Taylor." A paper delivered to the annual meeting of the Canadian Political Science Association, Quebec City, 29 May 2001.

Monière, Denis. 1983. *André Laurendeau et le destin d'un peuple*. Montréal: Québec/Amérique.

– 1990. "André Laurendeau et la vision québécoise du Canada." In Comeau and Beaudry 1990, 191–200.

Muggeridge, John. 1978. "George Grant's Anguished Conservatism." In Schmidt 1978, 40–8.

Nadeau, Jean-François. 1993. "Itinéraire de la pensée d'André Laurendeau (1912–1968)." *L'Action nationale* 83 (May): 645–58.

Noble, Richard. 1999. "Innis's Conception of Freedom." In Acland and Buxton 1999, 31–45.

O'Donovan, Joan E. 1984. *George Grant and the Twilight of Justice*. Toronto: University of Toronto Press.

Oliver, Michael. 1991a. *The Passionate Debate: The Social and Political Ideas of Québec Nationalism, 1920–1945*. Montréal: Véhicule Press.

– 1991b. "Laurendeau et Trudeau: leurs opinions sur le Canada." In *L'engagement intellectuel: mélanges en l'honneur de Léon Dion*. Sainte-Foy: Les Presses de l'Université Laval, 339–68.

Owram, Doug. 1986. *The Government Generation: Canadian Intellectuals and the State, 1900–1945*. Toronto: University of Toronto Press.

Panitch, Leo. 1995. "Elites, Classes and Power in Canada." In Michael Whittington and Glen Williams, eds., *Canadian Politics in the 1990s*, 3rd edition. Toronto: Nelson Canada, 182–207.

Panitch, Leo and Donald Swartz. 1985. *From Consent to Coercion: The Assault on Trade Union Freedoms*. Toronto: Garamond Press.

Reimer, A. James. 1978. "George Grant: Liberal, Socialist or Conservative?" In Schmidt 1978, 49–60.

Rioux, Marcel. 1951a. "Remarques sur l'éducation secondaire et la culture canadienne-française." *Cité libre* 1 (February): 34–42.

– 1951b. "Some Medical Beliefs and Practices of the Comtemporary Iroquois Longhouse of the Six Nations Reserve." *Journal of Washington Academy of Sciences* 41 (5): 152–8.

– 1953. "Remarques sur l'éducation secondaire." *Cité libre* 4 (November): 54.

– 1955a. "Idéologie et crise de conscience du Canada français." *Cité libre* 14 (December): 1–29.

– 1955b. "Notes autobiographiques d'un indien Cayuga." *Anthropologica* 1: 18–37.

– 1957. *Belle-Anse.* Ottawa: Musée national du Canada.

– 1960. "La démocratie et la culture canadienne-française." *Cité libre* 9 (June-July): 3–4, 13.

– 1961. "Socialisme, cléricalisme et Nouveau Parti." *Cité libre* 11 (January): 4–8.

– 1964. "Le socialisme aux U.S.A." *Socialisme* 64 (1): 87–107.

– 1965. "Conscience nationale et conscience de classe au Québec." *Cahiers internationaux de sociologie* 38 (January-June): 99–108.

– [1969a, 1977] 1987. *La question du Québec.* Montréal: L'Hexagone.

– 1969b. "Remarques sur la sociologie critique et la sociologie aseptique." *Sociologie et Sociétés* 1 (May): 53–67.

– 1974. *Les Québécois.* Paris: Seuil.

– 1977. "Le développement culturel." In Daniel Latouche, ed., *Premier mandat: une prospective à court terme du gouvernement péquiste.* Montréal: L'Aurore.

– 1978a. *Essai de sociologie critique.* Montréal: Hurtubise HMH.

– 1978b. "Ceux d'en haut et ceux d'en bas." *Possibles* 2 (Winter-Spring): 7–11.

– 1978–1979."Régions: nostalgie ou avant-garde." *Vie des arts.* 73 (93): 18–19.

– 1979. "Quelle éducation? Quelle culture?" *Possibles* 3 (Spring-Summer): 203–10.

– 1980a. "Le besoin et le désir d'un pays." *Possibles* 4 (Winter): 7–13.

– 1980b. "L'autogestion, c'est plus que l'autogestion." *Possibles* 4 (Spring-Summer): 15–22.

– 1981. *Pour prendre publiquement congé de quelques salauds.* Montréal: L'Hexagone.

– 1982. "Développement culturel et culture populaire." In Gilles Pronovost, ed., *Cultures populaires et sociétés contemporaines.* Québec: Les Presses de l'Université du Québec, 159–64.

– 1983. "La région incertaine." *Protée* 11 (Spring): 11–12.
– 1984. *Le besoin et le désir.* Montréal: L'Hexagone.
– 1985. "Sociologie critique et création artistique." *Sociologie et Sociétés* 17 (October): 5–11.
– 1986. "De l'Etat-Providence à l'Etat-Provigo." *Possibles* 10 (Spring-Summer): 29–39.
– 1990a. *Un peuple dans le siècle.* Montréal: Boréal.
– [1979] 1990b. "Un écrivain et son pays." In *Un peuple dans le siècle.* Montréal: Boréal 407–32.
– 1990c [1975]. "Les intellectuels et la liberté." In *Un peuple dans le siècle*, 433–46.

Rioux, Marcel and Jacques Dofny. [1962] 1972. "Les classes sociales au Canada français." In Marcel Rioux and Yves Martin, eds., *La société canadienne-française.* Montréal: Hurtubise HMH, 315–24.

Rioux, Marcel, Yves Lamarche et Robert Sévigny, eds. 1973. *Aliénation et idéologie dans la vie quotidienne des Montréalais francophones.* 2 vols. Montréal: Les Presses de l'Université de Montréal.

Rioux, Marcel, Hélène Loiselle, François Loranger, Claude Jutra, Léon Bellefleur, Laurent Bouchard, and Gérald Godin. 1975. "Rapport du Tribunal de la culture." In *Liberté*, 101 (December): 4–85.

Rioux, Marcel and Susan Crean. 1980. *Deux pays pour vivre: un plaidoyer.* Montréal: Les Éditions Saint-Martin.

Ryan, Claude. 1990. "Il a soulevé les vraies questions et réfuté les réponses toute faites." In Comeau and Beaudry 1990, 277–81.

Ryerson, Stanley Bréhaut. 1990. "Laurendeau, la Commission royale, l'histoire." In Comeau and Beaudry 1990, 219–22.

Salter, Liora. "'Public' and Mass Media in Canada: Dialectics in Innis's Communication Analysis." In Melody, Salter, and Heyer 1981, 193–208.

Salter, Liora and Cheryl Dahl. 1999. "The Public Role of the Intellectual." In Acland and Buxton 1999, 114–134.

Scott, F.R. 1957. "W.L.M.K." In F.R. Scott and A.J.M. Smith, eds., *The Blasted Pine.* Toronto: Macmillan, 27–8.

Siegfried, André. 1966. *The Race Question in Canada.* Toronto: McClelland and Stewart.

Schmidt, Larry, ed. 1978. *George Grant in Process: Essays and Conversations.* Toronto: Anansi Press.

Smiley, Donald. 1967. *The Canadian Political Nationality.* Toronto: Methuen

Spry, Irene. 1999. "Economic History and Economic Theory: Innis's Insights." In Acland and Buxton 1999, 105–13.

Stamps, Judith. 1999. "Innis in the Canadian Dialectical Tradition." In Acland and Buxton 1999, 46–66.

Taylor, Charles. 1970. *The Pattern of Politics*. Toronto: McClelland and Stewart.

– 1982. *Radical Tories: The Conservative Tradition in Canada*. Toronto: Anansi Press.

– 1985a. *Human Agency and Language*. Vol. 1 of *Philosophical Papers*. New York: Cambridge University Press.

– 1985b. *Philosophy and the Human Sciences*. Vol. 2 of *Philosophical Papers*. New York: Cambridge University Press.

– 1985c. "Atomism." In *Philosophy and the Human Sciences*, 187–210.

– 1985d. "What's wrong with negative liberty?" In *Philosophy and the Human Sciences*, 211–29.

– 1985e. "Legitimation Crisis?" In *Philosophy and the Human Sciences*, 248–88.

– 1985f. "Kant's Theory of Freedom." In *Philosophy and the Human Sciences*, 318–37.

– 1989. *Sources of the Self: The Making of the Modern Identity*. Cambridge, MA: Harvard University Press.

– 1991. *The Malaise of Modernity*. Concord, ON: House of Anansi.

– 1992. *Multiculturalism and the Politics of Recognition*. Princeton, NJ: Princeton University Press.

– 1993. *Reconciling the Solitudes: Essays on Canadian Federalism and Nationalism*. Ed. Guy Laforest. Montreal: McGill-Queen's University Press.

– 1995. *Philosophical Arguments*. Cambridge, MA: Harvard University Press.

Tocqueville, Alexis de. [1835] 1994. *Democracy in America*. New York: Alfred A. Knopf.

Trudeau, Pierre Elliott. 1968. *Federalism and the French Canadians*. Toronto: Macmillan of Canada.

– 1970a. *La Grève de l'amiante*. Montréal: Éditions du jour.

– 1970b. *Approaches to Politics*. Toronto: Oxford University Press.

– 1972. *Trudeau en direct*. Montréal: Éditions du jour.

Trudeau, Pierre Elliott and Thomas S. Axworthy. 1990. *Towards a Just Society*. Markham, ON: Viking.

Underhill, Frank. 1960. *In Search of Canadian Liberalism*. Toronto: Macmillan.

Westfall, William. "The Ambivalent Verdict: Harold Innis and Canadian History." In Melody, Salter, and Heyer 1981, 37–52.

Whitaker, Reginald. 1983. "'To Have Insight Into Much and Power Over Nothing': The Political Ideas of Harold Innis." *Queen's Quarterly* 90 (Autumn): 818–31.

Index